CONTAINER
VEGETABLE GARDENING

HOW TO HARVEST WEEK AFTER WEEK, EVERYTHING YOU NEED TO KNOW TO START GROWING PLANTS, FRUITS AND HERBS FOR ALL SEASONS IN A SMALL SPACE AT HOME, VEGETABLES

LISA EDWARD

© Copyright 2020 by Lisa Edward -All right reserved.

The work contained herein has been produced with the intent to provide relevant knowledge and information on the topic on the topic described in the title for entertainment purposes only. While the author has gone to every extent to furnish up to date and true information, no claims can be made as to its accuracy or validity as the author has made no claims to be an expert on this topic. Notwithstanding, the reader is asked to do their own research and consult any subject matter experts they deem necessary to ensure the quality and accuracy of the material presented herein.

This statement is legally binding as deemed by the Committee of Publishers Association and the American Bar Association for the territory of the United States. Other jurisdictions may apply their own legal statutes. Any reproduction, transmission or copying of this material contained in this work without the express written consent of the copyright holder shall be deemed as a copyright violation as per the current legislation in force on the date of publishing and subsequent time thereafter. All additional works derived from this material may be claimed by the holder of this copyright.

The data, depictions, events, descriptions and all other information forthwith are considered to be true, fair and accurate unless the work is expressly described as a work of fiction. Regardless of the nature of this work, the Publisher is exempt from any responsibility of actions taken by the reader in conjunction with this work. The Publisher acknowledges that the reader acts of their own accord and releases the author and Publisher of any responsibility for the observance of tips, advice, counsel, strategies and techniques that may be offered in this volume.

TABLE OF CONTENTS

Introduction 1

Chapter 1: The Many Advantages of Creating Your Own Garden 4

    You Will Be Saving a Heap of Money in the Long-Run 5
    You Know Exactly Where Your Food is Coming From 6
    You Can Hand-Pick Exactly What Variety of Produce You Need 6
    You Get to Grow Your Own Food, and it's Healthier! .. 7
    You can avoid GMOs 8
    Gardening is Meditative 9
    It is Better for the Environment 10
    If You Have Kids, Gardening is a Great Learning and Bonding Experience 10

Chapter 2: Healthy Eating Benefits 12

    You Will Develop a Better Immunity Against Disease 13
    Healthy Food Has More Nutrients 14
    You Will Have Improved Cognition and Memory 15
    You Can Achieve and Maintain a Healthy Weight 16
    You Will Have a Better Mood 16
    It Gives You More Energy 17
    You'll Develop a Better Self-Esteem 18
    It Can Prevent Certain Chronic Conditions and Diseases 19
    You Can Build Stronger Teeth and Bones 20
    It Reduces the Risk of Cancer 20
    The Bottom Line 21

Chapter 3: Getting Started 22

Chapter 4: Planning Your Space – Create a Map 24

Chapter 5: Container Gardening Tips and Tricks 28

    Keep a Gardening Journal 28

    Make a Watering Schedule 29

    Choosing the Best Lighting for Each Plant 30

    Choosing the Best Soil 31

    Get Creative With Your Containers! 32

    Plan Around Your Environment and Climate 33

    Save Your Seeds! 34

    Fertilizer is Your Friend 38

    Crafty Container Placement 39

    Quick Harvesting and Storage Tip 40

Chapter 6: Which Plants Do Well in Containers? 42

    'Fruit' Vegetables 43

        Tomatoes 43

        Bell Peppers 45

        Chili Peppers 48

    Root Vegetables 50

        Radishes 50

        Beets 54

        Onions 57

        Garlic 59

    Leafy Greens 63

        Spinach 63

        Lettuce 66

        Kale 68

    Pole Beans 71

  Green Beans 71
 Herbs 75
  Basil 76
  Oregano 76
  Sage 77
  Parsley 77
  Peppermint 77
  Rosemary 78
 Fruit 79
  Berries 79
  Cherries 80
  Figs 81
  Plums 82
  In Conclusion 83

Chapter 7: Different Volume Containers 84

 Shrubs and Trees 85
 Large or Climbing Fruits and Vegetables 85
 Herbs and Greens 85
 Grouped Fruits and Veggies 86

Chapter 8: Growing and Harvesting Vegetable Garden & Fruits Container 88

 Cultivating Your Container Garden 89
  Preparing the Soil 89
  Fertilization 94
  Sowing/Planting 95
  Succession Planting 97
  Watering 99
  Harvesting 101

Storing 103

Chapter 9: Accessories and Tools 105

Containers 106

Gardening Gloves 107

Garden Shears, Pruner, or Scissors 108

Dibber or Small, Narrow Stick 108

Mesh Sieve or Window Screen 109

Mason Jars, Paper Bags, and Ziplock Bags 109

String, Yarn, or Twine 110

Watering Can or Hose... 110

Spade or Trowel 111

Three-Pronged Fork, or Hand Cultivator 111

Wooden Stakes or Trellises...................................... 111

Labeling Stakes, Paint, Markers, and/or Labeling Tape
.... 112

Kneeling Pad or Soft Towel..................................... 113

Tool Care Tips 113

Chapter 10: Vegetable & Fruit Guide Per Season 115

Plant 116

   Winter 116

   Spring... 116

   Summer.. 117

   Fall 118

Harvest 119

   Winter 119

   Spring... 119

   Summer.. 120

   Fall 121

Chapter 11: The Right Pot for Every Plant 123

The Classic Clay Pot 125
Metal Containers 126
Fiberglass Containers 127
Fiberstone Containers... 128
Polystyrene Foam 129
Resin Containers 129
Wooden Containers... 130
Fabric Containers 131
Ceramic Containers 132
Concrete Containers 133
Hypertufa Containers 134
Fiber-lined Containers.. 134
Plastic Containers... 136
Miscellaneous and Unique Containers...................... 137
Parameters to Consider 138
    Drainage... 138
    Durability... 139
    Weight and Mobility 139

Chapter 12: Selecting Seeds 140

Create a Plan 140
Choosing the Right Seeds 142
Storing Your Seeds 146

Chapter 13: Protecting Your Plants 148

Weeds.. 148
Weather 149
    Frost 149
    Drought... 150

    Heavy Rain, Wind, and/or Thunderstorms 151
Animals 151
General Tiny Insects and Pests 153
Hornworm Infestations 155
    Handpicking 156
    Planting Basil 157
    Introducing Ladybugs 158

Chapter 14: How to Harvest 159

'Fruit' Vegetables 160
Pole Beans 161
Root Vegetables 161
Leafy Greens 163
Herbs 164
Berries 165
Fruit 166
Drying out Your Herbs and Small Vegetables 167

Chapter 15: Maintaining Your Vegetable Garden Year After Year 169

Mulch is a Wonderful Thing 169
Remove Dead Plants and Debris 170
Check Up on Your Plants Often 171
Utilize Crop Rotation 172
Clean and Maintain Your Tools and Containers Every Year 173
Read Over Your Gardening Journal and Learn From it 174
Pruning is Critical 174
End the Year with a Nutrition Boost 175

Chapter 16: Plant Aromatic Herbs for Your Kitchen 176

Start with Plants, Not Seeds 177
Pick the Right Containers 178
Group the Herbs in Your Kitchen By Their Needs ... 179
Growing Herbs in Your Kitchen Allows You to Harvest as Needed 179
Hang Herbs in Your Kitchen to Dry Before Storing . 180
The Best Herbs for Your Kitchen Containers 180
- Basil 181
- Bay 181
- Chives 182
- Dill 182
- Oregano 182
- Parsley 183
- Peppermint 183
- Sage 184

Chapter 17: Problem Solving and FAQs 185

What Is Container Gardening? 185
Can I Use Any Container for my Garden? 186
If I Don't Like My Container After a While, Can I Move my Plant to a New Container? 187
Is PH Level Important in a Container Garden? 187
Can I use Dirt from my Yard in my Container Garden? 188
Can I Water my Plants on the Same Schedule? 189
Should I Line my Containers with Rocks or Other Materials? 189
Can I Have an Inside Container Garden? 190

What are Some Common Container Gardening Mistakes? 191

Conclusion 192

INTRODUCTION

Welcome to *Book Title*, where you can learn how to perfect your container-gardening skills. Thank you for choosing this book, as it was carefully brought together for your gardening needs. This book is chock-full of useful gardening tips, tricks, guides, lists, and more, so by the end of this book, you could be a container gardening expert!

I certainly hope you enjoy reading and learning all that container gardening has to offer you, for it is a journey of plentiful produce and bushels of excitement! In this book, we will be discussing all that you need to know to master the art of container gardening in an environment that is suitable for your unique needs! We will begin by outlining the many advantages of creating your own garden, and we will highlight the many benefits of eating healthy foods! Then, we will dive right in and get started with some container gardening basics!

After we get through the orientation process of introducing container gardening, we will get into the exciting process of mapping out and planning your container garden's layout with the space you have. After that, I'll give you a comprehensive list of plants that make great starting points for any container garden, complete with a wide variety of veggies, herbs, and greens inclusive enough to fit any gardener's needs!

Next, we'll talk about the different volumes of containers that are generally used in the gardening world, then we will go over some guidelines for growing and harvesting your container-bound produce! Once we get that out of the way, we'll go into a comprehensive list of all the tools you'll need to take the gardening world by storm!

Have I caught your interest yet? If not, how about an easy-to-follow guide on planting crops by the season, as well as a guide for choosing the perfect container for each of your precious plants? After we find the right container, we'll dive right into finding the perfect seeds for the sowing season!

Next up is the nitty-gritty of plant protection. There, we will go over the best ways to protect your produce from bugs, weather, animals, weeds, and more! Once we cover that, we will go into a more in-depth description of harvesting your tasty produce before proceeding to the chapter on maintaining your veggie garden through the years. This chapter will contain tips about companion planting, preventative pest control, whether or not to replant in the same spot, and more!

Our last two chapters will include a pleasing list of aromatic herbs for your kitchen and a problem-solving chapter full of frequently asked container gardening questions. I have extensively researched all of these chapters to give you quality content, for I wish you the best in all of your gardening endeavors! I hope you enjoy this book, and I assure you that every effort was made to uphold the greatest quality and the most thoughtful information possible. Happy reading, and happy gardening!

CHAPTER 1: THE MANY ADVANTAGES OF CREATING YOUR OWN GARDEN

Chances are that if you are reading this book you are already interested in gardening! Container gardening, and gardening in general, is an exciting and freeing experience that allows you to spend time with nature while getting your hands a little dirty. However, why don't I sweeten the deal by showing you all of the wonderful advantages that gardening can provide for your life? Dip your toes into the water of gardening, and you will quickly see what I mean!

You Will Be Saving a Heap of Money in the Long-Run

One of the greatest benefits of establishing your own garden is the money you save! You can grow your very own, personalized supermarket at your own home! For the same price as one tomato, or a cucumber, or head of lettuce, you can buy enough bulbs or seeds to make a whole bushel of veggies!

Additionally, if you take proper care of your garden, it will keep producing for months on end! You only have to buy the initial seeds, for the most part, then you can propagate, save seeds, and more to grow and reproduce your garden year after year! That definitely beats all those trips to the supermarket, now doesn't it?

Speaking of the supermarket, you will be saving a ton of gas money when you can simply walk into your back yard and pick your own lunch! Your wallet, and your monthly food bill, will thank you if you supplement your groceries with home-grown food!

You Know Exactly Where Your Food is Coming From

When you grow your own food, you know exactly where it came from and who touched it. You can oversee its growth, ensure that no pests get to it, and ensure that it's not jostled around during harvest. It takes a burden off your shoulders when the veil of mystery is lifted regarding what you are putting into your body. Your food will go straight in the ground, come sprouting up, and make its way right from your container garden to your kitchen table!

You Can Hand-Pick Exactly What Variety of Produce You Need

Gardening is a great way to hand-pick, literally, what you put into your body. You can add a large variety of veggies and greens to your table, and your body will thank you! Many home-grown fruits, veggies, herbs, and greens are packed with much more nutrients than store-bought produce that has been sitting on the shelves for days to weeks at a time. You will also diversify your diet in a way that ensures you get all the nutrients you need for a healthy life.

The raw, fresh veggies and produce you grow in your own home will reward you with better flavors, richer nutrients, and better shelf lives than anything you can get at the store, and you can choose exactly which varieties fit your lifestyle best! Many types of crops you can grow at home are hard to find at the grocery store, and you can make sure that you have exactly what you need when you need it.

You Get to Grow Your Own Food, and it's Healthier!

There are very few things as exciting as creating things on your very own. What's better? You get to grow your very own food! You are in charge of what you grow, how much, and how often! Home-grown food tastes so much better than store-bought, too! You will always get to eat fresh and wholesome food that is not contaminated by the hands and shelf-life of the grocery-store world.

Home-grown food is much healthier than much store-bought produce due to how fresh it is when you pick it. When you buy a tomato from the grocery store, that tomato likely spent days or weeks on a truck as it was shipped across the country. Then, it spends more days and weeks sitting in the grocery store. During its life at the store, many hands touched it, it lost much of its nutritional value, and it won't taste as good!

After reading that, who wouldn't want to cultivate their own crops? Take care of your own health and wellbeing by becoming in charge of your food and your life!

You can avoid GMOs

GMOs are genetically modified organisms. They are normally seen in commercially-processed foods, such as fruits, vegetables, snack items, and more. When you create your own garden, you can grow your food organically and avoid eating something that is modified to its core. Additionally, by planting your fruits and veggies from organic, or non-GMO seeds, you are getting much more out of your crops. Generally, GMO foods have half the nutritional value of organic foods. This means that naturally-grown food, in your own home, is packed with more vitamins, minerals, and micronutrients than anything you can buy in most stores. It also allows you to avoid the high costs of buying organic produce when you can grow it yourself for a fraction of the cost!

Gardening is Meditative

Gardening is a very relaxing hobby, and it can bring a peaceful solution to your daily stresses. Spending time outside in the fresh air, away from all the hustle and bustle of life, is one of the world's greatest treasures. Caring for something like a plant is also very therapeutic, as it gives you a sense of control and responsibility that is very rewarding in the end.

Gardening is also a great workout, actually. Boost your health with some plant-tending and a hefty helping of elbow grease, and you will feel empowered and healthy in no time! All that planting, digging, weed-pulling, mulching, and watering can really work up a sweat and burn as many as four-hundred calories per hour! Talk about a great workout. Working out helps improve the mood and give a sense of contentment to your body, so it is a wonderful boost to your spirit and your health.

Additionally, sunshine is a great mood-booster, and it will give you some much-needed vitamin D, which helps with calcium production and retention in the body. You will feel much happier, and much more rejuvenated, after a few hours outside in the garden.

It is Better for the Environment

Gardening sustainably is wonderful for the environment. You are cultivating oxygen-producing plants while cutting down on the emission of greenhouse gasses by cutting the trips to the supermarket. Adding some greenery to your home is a great way to give back to the earth and bask in its bountiful glory.

In addition to cutting down on greenhouse gasses, you are also positively impacting the earth by cutting down on store-bought produce purchases. When big produce trucks have to transport crops across the country, it sucks up needless amounts of fossil fuels and spouts tons of greenhouse gasses into the atmosphere. When you make your own food, less food, marginally, has to be transported throughout the years. It may be a small difference, but it definitely matters to planet Earth.

If You Have Kids, Gardening is a Great Learning and Bonding Experience

Set your kiddos up for a prosperous and lively future by introducing them to gardening at a young age, or any age for that matter! Gardening will open up their minds, hearts, and imaginations in many ways! Plus, what kiddo doesn't like getting his or her hands dirty? They will learn important skill sets that they can carry into adulthood, get some fresh air, and spend time with their favorite person! You can become a great role model for your child as they watch you work hard at something that produces amazing results for you and your family!

Gardening is a wonderful bonding experience, and it gives you a great outlet for spending some exciting, fun time with your little ones so they can create meaningful memories. They will also gain a sense of pride as they help create something as wonderful as their own fruits and veggies! They will get a great mood boost, plenty of sunshine, and greater self-esteem as they grow plants of their very own.

CHAPTER 2: HEALTHY EATING BENEFITS

The benefits of eating healthily, especially when aided by your own garden, are plentiful. Feel happier, stronger, smarter, and full of life with a diet packed with whole grains, raw fruits and veggies, home-grown leafy greens and herbs, and more! Living off the land, and off a nutrient-packed diet, will give you a boost of health that will follow you for your entire life!

You Will Develop a Better Immunity Against Disease

When you eat a diet full of vitamin-rich produce, you get a big immunity boost. Produce like tomatoes, oranges, and more have vitamin C, B12, and other vitamins that boost your immunity and your body. This will give you the power you need to fight off any disease that life throws at you!

In addition to healthy vitamins and minerals, did you know that a diet full of lean proteins can give you as much protection against diseases as anything else? Eating protein keeps your body strong, and it gives your immune system a big boost as well!

Furthermore, foods that are full of flavonoids have many anti-viral and immune-boosting properties as well. Foods that have antibacterial and antiviral properties include freshly-brewed green tea, vitamin C-packed citrus fruits, kaempferol-filled leafy greens such as spinach, healthy oleuropein-filled oils like olive oil, and fibrous veggies like onions, broccoli, and apples! Many spices, as well, aid in the reduction of diseases. Spices such as these include chili powder, oregano, turmeric, powdered garlic, rosemary, and ginger root! There are many disease-fighting whole foods out there, so give any of them a try for a healthy, powerhouse of an immune system!

Aside from antiviral and antibacterial foods, your gut's health plays a big factor in your immune system as well! Probiotic-filled foods such as fermented kimchi and sauerkraut give your stomach's microbiome a boost. Apples, flaxseed, and seaweed also aid in the health of your stomach and bowels! A large majority of your immune health lies in your digestive tract, so take good care of it for optimal immune health and longevity!

Healthy Food Has More Nutrients

Whole foods such as fruits, veggies, greens, and wholegrains are packed with nutritious vitamins and minerals that will keep your body running at optimal levels. Produce is filled with fiber that will keep your bowels in order and your stomach satisfied. Greens are filled with blood-boosting iron. Fruits are jam-packed with vitamins such as vitamins A, C, and E that will keep your body running smoothly. Nuts are full of protein and calcium for your muscles and bones, and many fruits and root vegetables are filled with antioxidants that will fight off the free radicals that want to wreak havoc on your cells. Whatever the whole food you choose, there is a wonderful benefit to be acquired.

You Will Have Improved Cognition and Memory

The healthier you eat, the stronger your brain will be! Whole foods are packed with brain-improving nutrients like omega-3 fatty acids, vitamins, and minerals! Blueberries, fresh tea made from home-grown herbs, and more will give you a boost of brain activity and clarity! Keeping your mind sharp is as easy as staying hydrated and boosting your systems with all the natural vitamins and minerals that you need! Keep yourself from getting sluggish and forgetful, and fill your plate and belly with home-grown produce. When you start eating right, your brain will function on a whole other level!

There is a lot of truth behind the mind-body connection, so when you have a well-running body, your mind will follow suit and vise versa. Provide a stable foundation for a healthy brain by building up the strongholds of your body. Additionally, your body houses your mind, and you'd want a stable and healthy home just like your brain does, right? Eat healthily and you can achieve this with minimal roadblocks!

You Can Achieve and Maintain a Healthy Weight

A diet full of unhealthy fats, sugars, and processed foods can lead to harmful weight gain, so when you switch to a healthy diet, rich in protein and fiber, you will be able to lose and maintain weight at a better rate. Unnatural sugars pack on the pounds, but you can satisfy your sweet tooth with lots of fibrous fruits for a vitamin-filled, healthy dessert.

The great thing about whole foods is that they are generally lower in calories than processed foods. Unnatural foods are packed with added sugars, additives, and sodium that will leave you bloated and steadily gaining weight to no end. Whole foods are filled with fiber, water, vitamins, and minerals that will steadily melt the weight right off and keep you full for hours. You will be much happier and much lighter when you switch to a healthy diet, I assure you!

You Will Have a Better Mood

There is a big connection between the food you eat and your mood. For instance, sugary foods that spike your blood sugar leave you with fatigue and gloomy moods. Fruits and veggies high in fiber and vitamins such as vitamin C, however, can make you feel more cheery and energetic! It's all about what you eat.

There has also been a connection between food and mental stability and disorders. When you don't eat the nutrients you need, your mood and brain function start to fall to the wayside. You can also develop depression and other mental health issues, including impaired memory if you don't supply your body and brain with what they need. Survival is as much about the brain as it is the body, so keep both sharp and strong in order to live your best life!

It Gives You More Energy

It goes without saying that food gives people energy, but did you know that whole foods and healthy produce gives you more sustainable energy? Simple carbs and processed foods give you energy for the moment, but fibrous, protein-rich, and nutrient-rich foods will help you last a whole day with all the vitality you need! Complex carbohydrates also give you folic acid and a full belly, which will keep you satiated and happy.

Another important step to maintaining your energy is to eat small, frequent meals throughout the day to maintain your energy levels. Big, calorie-packed meals once or twice a day will leave you feeling bloated, and you will feel hungry and fatigued for the rest of the day. Keep up your energy reserves with plenty of protein, fiber, healthy oils, veggies, and complex carbohydrates to feel your best and conquer the day!

You'll Develop a Better Self-Esteem

Losing weight, boosting your mood, and maintaining your energy levels with healthy eating will make your self-esteem skyrocket. When you know you have a healthy, well-functioning body, it makes you feel much better about yourself and your life in general. Knowing you've accomplished having a beneficial and healthy life will improve your mood and give you a better outlook on the days to come.

Many people say that self-esteem starts with the body. That, I believe, is very true. In order to be happy and proud of yourself, you have to be happy and proud of the vessel that you are in! When you take good care of your body, you feel a sense of accomplishment, and when you get that body into a healthy rhythm and down to a manageable weight, it will make you feel on top of the world!

It Can Prevent Certain Chronic Conditions and Diseases

By eating healthy, you are safeguarding your body against chronic conditions such as heart disease, high blood pressure, and type 2 diabetes. By replacing unnatural sugars with natural sugar and fiber-filled fruits, you are already well on your way to reducing your risk of these conditions. Furthermore, whole foods don't have added salts that lead to higher blood pressures that lead to heart disease. Pair that with healthy fats that don't pad the arteries, and you are good to go!

Whole foods also help maintain and manage your blood glucose levels, reducing your overall risk for developing type 2 diabetes. They also keep you full so you don't binge on harmful, unhealthy snack foods! The vitamin E in healthy nuts and seeds has also been linked to the reduction and prevention of stroke-causing blot clots! Foods such as sunflower seeds, almonds, and peanuts are the name of the game. All in all, a healthy diet is the best way to prevent and manage many chronic conditions and diseases.

You Can Build Stronger Teeth and Bones

Calcium and vitamin D-rich foods prevent poor bone density and potential osteoporosis later in life. They fortify your bones and give you the strength and hardiness you need to get through a vibrant life! Additionally, magnesium-rich nuts, greens, and whole-grains keep your bones healthy and stout! Fill your belly with food like broccoli, sunflower seeds, almonds, cabbage, and legumes, and you will have plenty of magnesium and calcium to power through your day with ironclad strength!

It Reduces the Risk of Cancer

When you eat a diet rich in whole foods and natural sugars, you reduce your risk of cancer. Many processed and artificial foods are full of carcinogens that can wreak havoc on your body. Therefore, switching to a healthier lifestyle will protect you from a lot of the worry behind developing cancer.

Furthermore, many fruits and veggies are filled with phytochemicals and antioxidants that protect from cancer-causing free radicals in the body. They will also boost your overall immune system and strength, helping you fight against cancer before it becomes an issue.

Not to mention, a healthy diet of rich fruits, veggies, and whole foods helps to maintain your weight. Obesity has been linked to a higher risk of cancer, so eating healthy and losing some extra pounds can help you fight against potential tumors.

The Bottom Line

Now that you know the what, how, and why behind healthy eating, you can take the world by storm! With a strong and vibrant body, and a diet full of healthy, whole foods, you can rest assured that your days will be filled with plentiful nutrients that you need. Take this into account when choosing plants for your garden, and you can be growing a powerhouse of nutrition in no time!

CHAPTER 3: GETTING STARTED

Now that you know all of the benefits you can receive once you start gardening and eating healthy foods, let's dive right into how you can get your container gardening journey started! Later in this book, we will showcase a more in-depth description surrounding the tools you will need, general tips and tricks, your planned growing space, your potential plants, and containers you can use. However, in this chapter, we'll address getting started with your new container garden!

In short, the best thing about creating a container garden of your very own is that it is available to anyone! Anybody can do container gardening if they want to, regardless of where you live! It's like a mobile, portable garden that is fully customizable to your needs! The size of the container garden is up to you, depending on your available space, but that is the beauty of it! A container garden can be just a few small herbs on your window sill, a whole sunny room in your home dedicated to growing tomatoes, a balcony spilling over with gorgeous leaves and fruits, or even a spacious outdoor garden that fills the yard with pots, jars, barrels, and kitchen sinks full of edible goodies! The choice is yours, and that is amazing.

Getting started, you need to assess your space and see what size and type of garden you can pursue. Then, you can get creative and pick out all of the wonderful containers you get to choose for your endeavors. The possibilities are truly endless! You can go with the simplistic, clay-pot garden, or you can go all-out with painted, decorated odds and ends that can be filled with your plants of choice. Pick out your garden spots, fill them with containers, and then pick out your favorite fruits and veggies, perfectly suited for your lifestyle.

Get a plan together in your head, and a general idea for your garden and how you want it positioned, then use this book as a guide to take you through the steps of your gardening journey. Soon, you will be able to grow and cultivate the container garden of your dreams!

All it takes is a little bit of imagination, some planning, and a pinch of knowledge, and you can create something absolutely amazing that will produce the best crops for you. Dive into the pages of this book and figure out exactly what you can plant in your unique container garden, and learn all that you need to know in order to maintain your garden and reap the benefits for years to come!

CHAPTER 4: PLANNING YOUR SPACE – CREATE A MAP

Though many containers can be moved around, it's a good idea to plan out a starting point for your container garden. Having a bigger picture, or a map, to work with makes cultivating and maintaining your garden much easier. It is a great idea to start out with a concept sketch of the area, or areas, in which you want to place your container garden before you purchase any plants. You can use a gardening journal, a spare piece of paper and a pencil, a computer program, or any medium that is comfortable for you to complete this plan and give you a visual. This will give you a good starting point to build off of.

Once you have a general idea in your head for the layout of your garden, and you begin purchasing seeds and plants, make a list of all the plants and seeds. Then, carefully label your sketch or diagram with the seeds and plants, giving each a designated area depending on their lighting needs. Move by section if going seed-by-seed or plant-by-plant is a bit scattered.

First, look at the sunniest places on your diagram to label tomatoes, peppers, strawberries, or other sun-loving plants. Then, go for the shady areas and log plants that prefer that, such as tart cherries. Then, map out places with trellises, fences, and/or walls for climbing varieties such as beans. Go space by space and purpose by the purpose of a well-rounded idea of what and where you would like to plant. This makes it easier to avoid mistakes and to avoid leaving anything out. Generally, when things have a specific purpose or need, they are easier to remember and plan accordingly.

If you plan to change out plants throughout the seasons, it is a good idea to color-code your labels. For instance, you can label summer plants with red, autumnal plants with orange, spring plants with green, and winter plants with blue in the same spaces to see what you will be planting during which seasons. This allows for great visuals and avoids overlapping and confusion. It also helps if you plan to do succession planting.

Doing a general map or plan every year, and keeping up with a gardening journal, will help you plan for the next year and all the years ahead. It will help you keep up with things that worked well for you, and it will allow you to learn from past mistakes so you can do better going forward. Planning everything out and keeping a detailed log is one of the best ways to make the most of your gardening experience year after year.

You can also make a general table, organized by plant type and lighting needs. This is a bit simpler and not as tailored to your exact living space, but it gives you a good visual for what plants you plan to use and what way they will be grouped together. Pictured below is a rough idea of a gardening plan. You can always expand on it later, once you have a more detailed map of the gardening space laid out for you.

Tomatoes	Bell Peppers	Strawberries	Chili Peppers	*Sun-Loving Plants*
Green Beans	Pole Beans	Cucumbers	Cherry Tomatoes	*Climbing Plants*
Tart Cherries	Spinach	Kale	Lettuce	*Shade-Loving Plants*
Beets	Radishes	Onions	Garlic	*Root Vegetables*

This is a rough but concise example of a template that is simple to create and easy to use to get an idea for where you will be grouping your crops and how you can organize them for optimal use in your garden. You can group by lighting needs, maturation speeds, aesthetics, and more, but the most important aspect of a diagram is to target your own specific needs and ideas. There is no wrong answer here. It's just important to get your thoughts and ideas out onto paper, or a computer screen, so you have something to bounce off of.

Keep up your gardening plans each year to develop and hone your gardening capabilities. Over time, it will become more natural and will give you ease when you continue planting and cultivating your perfect container garden. You can add or subtract details as you see fit. This should give you a great starting point into your gardening journey!

CHAPTER 5: CONTAINER GARDENING TIPS AND TRICKS

Whether you are brand new to container gardening or a seasoned sower of seeds, there are many new things we can learn every day about our potted plants. Here are a few tips and tricks for container gardening to give you a boost of inspiration that will help you tackle many of your container gardening questions!

Keep a Gardening Journal

Gardening journals are a wonderful thing to keep around when you start to dabble in gardening. They help you log what plants do well every month, conditions that need to be avoided the next year, the watering schedules that work best for your plants, and so much more. Keeping a gardening journal year after year can help you predict and plan for future years. This will help you in the long-run and give you the insight you need to learn from past mistakes and build upon processes that have worked for your garden.

A gardening journal can be as simple or as complex as you like. Some like to sketch pictures of their plants and take notes next to the sketches. Some like to print out and past pictures, logging the times and conditions next to them. Others like bulleted lists, a calendar-like setup, and a plethora of other templates. Find what works best for you, and stick with it. You never know how many gardening secrets you can unlock and carry with you through the years!

Make a Watering Schedule

One of the biggest mistakes a gardener can make is watering all of your plants on the same schedule. All plants are different, and they all need different levels of care. For instance, plants with thinner leaves generally need to be watered more frequently, and plants with thicker leaves need to be watered less often. This is because thicker leaves can retain more water, thus allowing a plant to thrive for longer periods of time without being watered.

As a general rule, plants can be watered every other day, but this is not the case for every plant, and this is where many gardeners start seeing wilted plants. Either the plant has had too much water, or it hasn't had enough! Plants require a delicate balance, and their watering schedule is a large part of this balance.

Research the watering needs of each type of plant you decide to incorporate into your garden. Then, write out a watering schedule on your calendar for each plant so you never miss your watering days! You can even color-code it per plant to make it easier to follow. This will give you a great visual so you will never have to guess which plant needs water on which days. As an added bonus, you can mark out days on which it rains so you can save on water and stay on track.

If your water research comes up a bit short, the best rule of thumb with watering is to feel the soil. If the soil is damp, it does not need to be watered. If the soil is dry to the touch, it needs to be watered.

As for the time of day that is best for watering, the early morning and dusk are optimal. At these times, your garden is not being bombarded with sunlight, and the water will have time to get down to the roots without being evaporated by the heat and light of the sun.

Choosing the Best Lighting for Each Plant

Following the same general line of thought from my last point, it is not a good idea to treat each plant equally in regards to lighting. Every type of plant has unique lighting needs, so placing them all in the same lighting environment will not likely bode well for the outcome of your plants. Some plants require full sun, some need partial shade or sun, and some need complete shade.

Carefully research the lighting needs of each plant that you plan to include in your garden, and map out enough space in your yard for each type of plant you choose. Make sure that you have enough lighting and shade for the plants you want to grow before purchasing them. This ensures that no over-crowding occurs and makes sure that each plant has a place to rest in the sun and/or shade.

Choosing the Best Soil

Choosing the best soil for your plants is very important for the longevity and production of your garden. A good starting point is to *not* use soil from your own yard. You may think that all soil is suitable, especially if your own soil has perfectly growing plants in it; however, unprocessed soil can clump and become unsuitable for plants that will be cultivated in a container. Soil straight from the ground is naturally adapted to the environment you get it from, so it may not work well in the container garden setting.

The best thing to do would be to buy nutrient-rich commercial potting soil. This soil is specifically made for plants that will be in containers, and it is perfectly aerated for a container-bound life. Potting soil normally has attributes that help it aerate and retain nutrients in order to replace the natural processes of ground soil. These attributes include peat moss, perlite, manure, compost, and/or vermiculite. All of these add to the quality of the soil and make maintaining your container garden much easier.

An additional note to make pertains not to the quality of the soil but the amount. When potting your plants, make sure to leave at least an inch of air space above the soil in the pot to facilitate easier watering and suitable growing space for your plant.

Get Creative With Your Containers!

If your containers are starting to bore you after looking at them for days on end, spruce them up! You can give them a nice coat of paint, create pretty designs on the sides, come up with creative labeling ideas, and more! If you paint your containers, make sure to choose a good waterproof paint in case of rain. Additionally, it is a good idea to choose colors that are bright and vibrant, for this will help the containers reflect sunlight and prevent your plants from getting too hot during the day. The exception to this is if you live in a cooler environment, in which case darker paint may be best. Dark paint will absorb sunlight and help your plant retain heat.

Plan Around Your Environment and Climate

The climate and environment in which you live play a large part in the planning and cultivation of your container garden. Plants thrive in different situations depending on the environment in which they live. For example, if you live in a very warm and sunny climate, opt for lighter-colored containers so your plants can stay cool. The lighter color reflects sunlight much better than heat-absorbing dark colors, so your plants will not dry out or overheat as easily when paired with proper watering.

Alternately, if your environment is a bit cooler during your planting and growing seasons, opt for the darker-colored containers. These will retain heat due to their ability to better absorb sunlight and heat, so your plants won't be as susceptible to frost and cool winds.

Another good tip for hotter environments is to add mulch to your containers. Mulch helps your plants retain water during hot days and harsh sunlight. It will help keep them cool and hydrated after a day basking in the sun!

Additionally, in order to get the most benefits and the highest level of ease with your gardening experience, try to choose plants that are native to your climate. This will help you in the long-run as it will take less maintenance overall to maintain your garden. They will naturally adapt to your area's climate and require less overall attention.

Save Your Seeds!

A great way to save a bundle of money in your gardening endeavor is to save your seeds! It's incredibly easy to do, and it will make it easier to sustainably utilize your garden to its fullest potential over the years.

Tomatoes are one of the most popular container-grown vegetables, and thankfully they have some of the easiest seeds to save! Tomatoes that are ripe and rot-free are prime candidates for seed-saving, and just one tomato can give you a whole bunch of seeds! You can munch on some fresh tomatoes while harvesting the seeds out of a few extra tomatoes, and you will have even more tomatoes the next year at no extra cost! How amazing is that?

What's more amazing is how easy it is to save seeds, including tomato seeds! All you have to do is scoop the seeds out, lie them on a paper towel, pat them down to get the juice out, and then air dry them! Then, you can store them in an air-tight container for the next seed-sowing season! They can even last up to six years, so you can stockpile your seeds for years to come! This is true for almost every type of seed you can gain from a vegetable!

You can also ferment seeds, which is a bit more complicated but holds its own benefits. When you ferment seeds, it rids them of many potential seed-borne diseases. To ferment seeds, there are a few important steps you'll need to take:

1. Rinse your vegetables in water to get all of the dirt off.
2. Cut off any damaged parts of your vegetable.
3. Cut your vegetable open and either scoop out or squeeze out the juice, seeds, and pulp from within.

4. Dump all of the juice, seeds, and pulp into a container of your choice. Make sure you choose a container with a lid.
5. Make sure you do not add water instead of vegetable juice, as it will water down the solution and slow the fermentation process.
6. Close the container and let it sit for about three days. Don't let the container get too hot, for if it gets above 70 degrees Fahrenheit, it won't ferment as well.
7. Stir the contents of the container after three days to allow the pulp to get re-covered in the juices. Do this once or twice a day. This helps prevent the cultivation of mold.
8. After three more days, decant the contents by adding water around three times the volume of the contents in the container.
9. Pour out the pulp that sits atop the seeds, making sure not to pour out any of the seeds themselves.
10. Look out for sinking seeds and floating ones. Generally, the ones that are floating are not going to plant well, and the sinking ones will be more likely to grow.
11. Continue to add water and pour the pulp out until the seeds are generally clean.

12. Strain the seeds on a flat, fine-mesh sieve or in a mesh strainer. A flat sieve is better for getting more surface area to wash off the seeds, but if you do not have one a window screen will work as well.
13. Gently rinse any remaining goop off the seeds and spread them evenly over the flat surface of the sieve or screen. This will allow optimal air-drying.
14. Rub the underside of the screen or sieve with a dry cloth, or tap the sides to get any excess water off prior to setting it down.
15. Allow the seeds to dry for around five days in order to ensure that no moisture remains.
16. Once the seeds are completely dry, scoop them into a zip lock bag or an air-tight container for storage.
17. Store the bag of seeds in a dark, dry place to prevent the seeds from prematurely sprouting. Do not refrigerate or freeze them, as this will harm the quality of the seeds.
18. Label the bag with a marker or a piece of tape in order to remember which bag contains which type of seeds.

19. That's it! The seeds should store safely for years and can be used for your next sowing season!

Fertilizer is Your Friend

Fertilizing your plants as they need it is critical to keeping them alive. Unlike plants that live in the ground, plants that are in containers are more dependent on you for nutrients. Plants in the ground have greater access to bugs, earthworms, and dead matter that aerate the soil and provide it with nutrients. Fertilizing your container garden helps mimic the natural processes that they are missing out on.

Additionally, keeping your plant's soil properly fertilized allows for your plant to get more nutrients after watering. When you water plants in the ground, the soil can retain many of its nutrients; however, when you water plants that are in containers, nutrients leech out when the water drains from the container as there is nothing to absorb them quickly enough. Therefore, you must replenish those nutrients often.

Fertilization does not have to be done every day, for that can actually oversaturate your plant's roots and cause issues. Fertilize your plants every couple of weeks in order to maintain their nutrients after repeated waterings and they will graciously thank you for it by providing you with delicious fruits and herbs!

Crafty Container Placement

There are many nifty ways to get creative with the placement of your containers, so don't think that simply placing them on the ground is the only option. There are many innovative ways to get the most out of your container gardening experience. I'll show you some here in this chapter, but you can also use your imagination and come up with new ideas that have yet to be discovered! The possibilities are endless.

The first crafty container idea I would like to show you is the container platform. Simply find a pallet or a few concrete blocks and create a platform for your container. This will keep it up off the ground and safe from runoff, minor flooding, and some pests. It will also allow for better draining from the bottom when you water it, which prevents root rot.

Another, similar craft idea involves hanging your containers to suspend them above the ground in order to create better water drainage, protection from pests and floods, and more! This method will also allow your plant to grow bigger and let its vines and leaves hang lower. This will allow you to get more from your plant and allow it to flow naturally. It also gives easy access for harvesting, so that is always a plus! This crafty container placement looks very appealing as well, which adds pizazz to your lovely container garden!

My final crafty container idea involves mobility! By placing your container on a platform with wheels, you can easily move heavier containers. This allows for protection from heavy rain, movement with the shade throughout the day, easier harvesting, garden reorganization, and more!

Now that you have some nifty new container ideas, try them out for yourself and create your own! Explore all of the possibilities that container gardening has to offer!

Quick Harvesting and Storage Tip

With nearly every type of crop that you harvest, the way in which you clean and store them is very important. For most vegetables, greens, and herbs, you will need to clean them gently with a dry cloth to wipe away the dirt. In almost every case, it is a bad idea to wash them immediately with water. Rinsing your crops with water is not recommended until you are ready to eat or use them, as water will encourage mold and rot while the crop is in storage. Rather, keep them dry, nice and cool in the crisping bin of the refrigerator if they are fruits and vegetables, and hang fresh herbs, onions, chili peppers, and garlic up to dry. This will keep your crop clean and safe until you are ready to use it.

CHAPTER 6: WHICH PLANTS DO WELL IN CONTAINERS?

There are so many wonderful fruits, vegetables, and herbs out there for a gardener to cultivate, but many of them require the wide expanse of the earth to thrive. For those in a smaller living situation or who simply want to change things up in their garden for new benefits, container gardening is a great way to go. There are plenty of plants that will thrive in a container, you just have to know where to look! Here we'll go over a comprehensive list of some of the best plants for a luscious container gardening experience!

'Fruit' Vegetables

Tomatoes

Tomatoes are one of the most popular plants to choose for a container garden. They are also very easy to cultivate and harvest, so it's also a great plant for a budding gardener. These wonderful vegetables, or to be more specific, fruit that we consider vegetables, come in a wide variety of shapes and sizes, so it is not hard to find ones that are perfect for you!

Tomatoes are so popular for container gardeners, there have actually been varieties that were bred specifically for container gardening! That goes to show the true popularity of tomatoes in the container-gardening scene! One of the container-ready tomato varieties is called the Atlas Hybrid tomato, and it is a delicious and plump beefsteak tomato variety. They can crop tomatoes around one pound, and they are plentiful! There is also the sweet Bush Early Girl Hybrid variety and many more!

Tomato plants, in general, crop a lot of crops, and they are very adaptable to the container-gardening life! Even non-engineered tomatoes are perfect for containers. They are actually considered to be the most productive of potted vegetables, so you will have a plethora of tomatoes to enjoy in no time! They can crop enough tomatoes to last a whole season, and they can be used in so many recipes. They can be used in salsas, salads, soups, pasta dishes, and more! They go great with basil and many vegetables, so you can always find a use for these lovely fruit-veggies!

Tomatoes are particularly lively when placed in direct sunlight, and they need a pot depth of at least one foot. After that, they are very easy to care for! They need to be watered every other day or so, but the easiest way to determine their watering needs is to feel the soil. This is the case for almost all plants, in fact, so it will not be difficult to keep these crimson beauties alive and thriving! Simply water them when their soil gets dry, and you will have minimal problems.

Bell Peppers

Do you like salsa, stir fry, and shish-kabobs? If you answered yes to any of those questions, or if you like the simple taste of crisp, sweet bell peppers, then these delightful and colorful veggies may be right up your alley! Bell peppers are great for a budding container gardener, and they are easy to care for and maintain once you get the basics down. Give them a suitable environment, adequate lighting, and a healthy dose of water, and you will be well on your way to cultivating a bustling garden full of colorful, delicious peppers!

Peppers enjoy the warm sun and humid air, but they can be grown anywhere with the right conditions and a dedicated gardener! They do not handle the cold well, so keeping them in a warm, well-lit area is a must. You can also turn to a darker-colored container, such as a black or navy-blue pot, to give them a better venue for heat-retention. As long as you keep these beauties warm and happy, they will serve you well in whatever container you choose!

Peppers take a bit longer to grow to fruition than tomatoes, making them slightly less popular than the previous veggie we discussed, but they make up for it by giving you a satisfying crunch and plenty of crops once they mature. As an added bonus, collecting and reusing pepper seeds is *incredibly* easy to do so you can have a bundle of pepper seeds for the next sowing season with no strain on your budget! Peppers crop a lot of seeds inside their fruits, and they are incredibly easy to harvest. Just scoop them out, lay them on a paper towel to dry, and store them in an air-tight bag once they are completely dry! It doesn't get much simpler than that.

It may be a good idea to invest in a sturdy stake for your pepper plants so their heavy fruits don't bend and topple their vines. This is very inexpensive and will allow for faster growth, more crops, and less hassle in the long-run.

Bell peppers come in a large variety of shapes, colors, and sizes, so you have many wonderful options to choose from! They come in the classic green, yellow, and red colors, but there are also some unique specimens out there like the orange, purple, and brown bell peppers! A favorite among gardeners is the cheerfully yellow Canary Bell pepper. This one takes a bit longer to grow, but it crops large, sweet yellow peppers that will compliment many dishes!

Another common favorite is the Big Red. As the name suggests, this pepper is a vibrant red color with thick, plump flesh! This pepper also takes less time to grow, so it is very popular among gardeners.

Last but not least is the classic, the green California Wonder bell pepper. These peppers are absolutely scrumptious, and they can even be left on the vine to mature to a sweeter, red variety of pepper. It's the best of both worlds!

Keep in mind when you choose your pepper variety, you need not get discouraged if your peppers start out green. Nearly all bell pepper varieties start out with green fruit. This is great if you like green bell peppers, but the longer you let your peppers remain on the vine to ripen, the sweeter and more nutrient-rich they will become. This is a unique benefit that gardeners get with peppers because you can choose what sweetness level, coloration, and size you'd like your crop to become. The timing of your harvesting is largely up to you, and it is a rather freeing experience!

Whichever bell pepper variety you pick out of the rainbow of possibilities, they are all great choices for your container gardening needs!

Chili Peppers

Chili peppers, the hottest of container veggies, are plentiful and prosperous. They are often chosen by those who like to add a bit of spice to their cuisine and their gardens! Their small size makes them absolutely perfect for container gardening, and as long as you show them the love and care they need with an added bit of heat, they won't let you down! They thrive in the sun and in warm environments of around 70-80 degrees Fahrenheit.

Jalapenos are the favorite chili pepper in the bunch, but there are many types of hot chilis out there. There are Thai chili peppers, Poblano peppers, African Bird's Eye peppers, and more! Each one has its own heat index, color, size, and shape, so there is bound to be a perfect pepper out there for you! Many peppers even change color from green to red, yellow, orange, and even purple!

The key to chili peppers is the length of time you keep them on the vine! The longer they hang, the spicier they become! If you like a milder kick of spice, the less mature, green varieties may be up your alley. If you like a swift kick of the burning-hot flavor, leaving the pepper on the vine until it turns a rich, vibrant color could be the name of the game!

Watering your chili peppers is not a hard task, as they only need to be watered enough to keep them from wilting. Shoot for about an inch to an inch and a half of water per week, or simply water the plants when the top inch and a half of soil is dry.

You can pick your plentiful peppers after about eight weeks of sprouting, and then you can make buckets of tongue-scorching salsa all summer long! The peppers can be harvested as soon as they begin to crop crops, but it is up to you when to begin the harvest. You can pick them at any stage of their fruition depending on the level of spice you prefer. You may think these spicy peppers will keep you on your toes, but stay dedicated and they will bless you with a delicious bounty for months to come!

Store your peppers in the fridge for up to a week, or dry them out in the sun for months or years of spicy goodness! Whichever way you choose, you will surely be on your way to a pepper-filled bounty in no time!

Root Vegetables

Radishes

Radishes are a happy little root vegetable that will snuggle up and make any container into a home. Radishes are well adapted to any container size, even the smallest you can find! Sprinkle some seeds into a pot of your choice, or any container for that matter, and watch the magic happen! You'll have a bushel of reddish-and-white beauties in no time at all!

Radishes are a versatile and delicious root vegetable, and though they are a bit bitter at times, they pack a tasty punch in many dishes such as a nice, hearty salad! What's better? They are incredibly easy to grow, so they are absolutely perfect for container gardening. Whether you are a complete beginner to gardening or an expert, you can't go wrong with these colorful veggies!

These hearty root vegetables are best planted in the early spring and fall, and they will steadily crop delightfully crisp crops. Better yet, every single aspect of the radish is edible, so you won't have any radish-induced food waste! The greens and roots of the radish plant make for delicious additions to any salad or soup! They also make great additions to sandwiches, sautéed dishes, or steamed veggie plates! They provide a big vitamin C boost as well, so if you are health-conscious, these are a great addition to your kitchen!

Radishes come in a range of sizes, from the smaller Cherry Bell that is common in grocery stores to the giant Large Daikon which can grow up to two feet long! Radishes are split into three categories, depending on their placement in their season of growth. There are early radishes, suitably named for their aptitude to the earlier halves of spring and fall. Then there is the midseason variety of radish, sown from around May to August. Lastly is the aptly named late variety of radishes, so named for their late summer sowing season. They are often called winter radishes as well, for in warmer climates they can be sown in the winter.

Radishes can be placed in either a sunny or shady area, depending on which part of the radish you prefer the most. If you place your container in a shadier spot, the leaves will grow longer and the roots will be smaller. If you place the radishes in a sunnier area, the roots will be much plumper. It is all a matter of preference, but most prefer a sunnier spot for the hearty, crisp roots of the radish plant.

Radishes are fast growers, so you should have no problem cultivating a large amount of the vegetable in a small amount of time. You can continue to sew and grow radishes all season long if you like, and you can choose a variety of radishes in order to gain a root-vegetable bounty all year long!

The harvest and storage of radishes are quite easy. To harvest your radishes, simply pull them from the soil! To store them, clean off the dirt with a clean, dry cloth and store them in the refrigerator. For longer shelf life, it is best to store the leaves and roots separately from one another. When you are ready to use them, you can simply rinse them off and get to eating! Make sure not to wash your radishes unless you are about to consume them, for vegetables can grow mold and rot if left in a moist environment when stored. The leaves normally stay fresh for about three days, and the roots keep for up to a week after harvest if stored properly.

The only exception to this is the late, or winter, variety of radish. They can last a few weeks in the refrigerator with no harm.

Beets

Beets, the delicious and sweet cousin of radishes, are a dark and striking magenta color. They are commonly pickled, canned, and preserved, but they can be eaten in a large manner of ways. These colorful beauties are on-par with radishes in terms of container compatibility, and they love small spaces. They will be snug as a bug in a rug while growing in your container garden, they just need to be deep enough in the soil to flourish. They generally enjoy a depth of about one foot of soil, and they will reward you with large, delightfully-colored roots! Their earthy taste when raw and sweet taste when pickled with have your heart and taste buds pounding! Even better, they have delicious greens that taste and look like spinach. In fact, beets are related to the spinach plant!

Beets are jam-packed with nutrients, and they are a must-have for a healthy household if you enjoy the crisp taste of root veggies. They are filled with essential vitamins and minerals such as iron, potassium, vitamin C, folate, and manganese, and they have a heaping serving of fiber!

Beets love to bask in the sun, so make sure to place their container in a bright and sunny area of your property so they can flourish. They can tolerate a bit of shade in the early and late parts of the day, but for the most part, they require plentiful sunlight. They don't mind cool temperatures, however, which makes them perfect for the spring and fall. They can also resist frost to a moderate extent, which means they will likely survive through the winter in warmer areas of the world.

When preparing to sow your seeds, it is important to note that they do not germinate as easily as other seeds. Their tough exteriors make it a bit harder for them to sprout than soft-seeded vegetables. Never fear, however, for there are easy ways to overcome this obstacle. Simply place your seeds in a colander under warm running water, then let them sit for about thirty minutes before planting them in the soil. This will soften their shells enough to promote healthy germination and growth! You can also soak them in warm water for about an hour to get the same results. In reality, you can soak them for as long as half a day before sowing them, but either method works. It is a matter of personal patience and preference.

After you have sown your beet seeds, you need to water them. After that, watering is easy! Beets do not require as much water as other plants, and they only need to be watered sparsely throughout the week. They require about an inch of water per week, so watering them about twice a week should suffice. If it is particularly hot, or if there is a drought, you may want to water them every day to be safe. In any situation, whenever you water your beets, make sure the soil is completely dry before watering them again.

Beets can be harvested after just under two months, and they are as easy to harvest as most other root vegetables. Just pull them from the top and yank out their root. It's as simple as that! As for storage, the root of the beet plant has a longer shelf life than the greens, so it is best to separate the two into different plastic bags in your fridge. Wipe off any dirt with a dry cloth, and make sure not to wash them with water until you are ready to eat them in order to prevent rot and mold. Beet greens last for about a week before showing signs of withering, and beetroots last about a week longer in the fridge, and a month longer in a dry root cellar.

Onions

Onions are an absolute staple in most homes, and they do very well in containers! Green onions fare the best in a container garden, but with enough practice, any onions can be cultivated in your container garden. They are easy to care for and wonderful for giving you a bounty of crops that you can snatch from the pantry and use for a plethora of meals at your leisure.

Onions come in many shapes, sizes, and colors, so there is surely one out there for you! There are white onions, green onions, purple onions, and more! The most common onions for your kitchen needs are white and Vidalia onions, but red onions also do great in salads and many cold dishes. Whichever you prefer, you can't go wrong choosing it for your container gardening experience!

Onions are very sturdy crops to sow, and they can withstand many temperatures. They do not like frost, but their seeds can be sown while there is still a bit of chill in the air. They do very well in mild climates and temperatures, and they are pretty hardy. Onions can be planted as seeds or bulbs, depending on when you'd like to begin planting onions in your container garden.

Onions don't need constant watering, but they need to be watered once every day or two as seedlings and about twice a week as they begin to grow. If you live in a particularly hot and dry area, daily may be better, but it is not required. They take a little while to grow, but the bounty at the end is well worth the wait! Fertilizing them will help boost their growth as well, as they love the nitrogen content of many fertilizers. Fertilizing your onions every week or so is best for the continual growth and health of your onions.

Weeding is not much of a problem when you are container gardening, but keep your eye out for potential insects that may take a fancy to your onion crops. They are generally easy to irradicate, but you need to make sure to check every week for potential pests.

As for harvesting, onions are among the easiest crops to harvest. All you have to do is pull them out of the soil by their green or brown tops, and you will have plentiful, bulbous onions!

Garlic

Unless you're a vampire, garlic can make a tasty staple to your kitchen cuisine! These delightful bulbs make a great addition to many dishes, such as pasta, pizza, stir-fry, and more! These savory root vegetables are well-adapted to the container life, and they will make a tasty addition to your blooming container garden. Cured, dried, or pickled, it also has an amazingly long shelf life!

Growing garlic in containers allows for a lot of flexibility. If you're creative, you can even grow garlic year-round! It will also save space and allow for easy mobility for your garlic plants. With container gardening. You don't have to worry about weeding these plants, and watering is simple. You can even move the container into the rain on a cloudy day for supple watering. Durable plastic or rustic clay pots do the job well. Whichever you choose, aim for a lighter color to prevent the absorption of heat from the sun. This will keep your soil from getting excessively dry, and your garlic can stay cool.

Choose a container that is around ten inches deep to allow your garlic ample room to grow, and plant the cloves a few inches apart for best survivability. Garlic is grown most popularly through the propagation of cloves, and luckily this is a very easy process to master! It's as easy as purchasing a few cloves of garlic from the grocery store and propagating them that way, or you can buy them from a plant nursery. If you do propagate them, retain their papery skin to protect them from potential infections.

A great way to give your garlic the best head-start in life is to chill the bulbs or cloves in the refrigerator prior to planting them. This fosters faster growth for your root veggies, as garlic enjoys cooler temperatures. This is also why garlic does so well in cooler climates. You can plant your garlic in the late fall and allow them to chill out through the winter, and they will sprout must easier this way! They like to have at least a month and a half of exposure to chilly temperatures in order to sprout well. A temperature below 45 degrees Fahrenheit is favorable.

As I mentioned earlier, however, you can plant garlic at any time of year if you take the right steps. In lieu of planting in the winter, you can keep your garlic cloves wrapped in a paper bag in the refrigerator for two to three months to allow them to chill before planting them. This allows you to mimic colder weather and cultivate your garlic in the comfort of your own home!

Once your cloves start to develop their root systems and begun to sprout, make sure they have plenty of sunlight and water them with about one inch of water per week to ensure lively, prosperous garlic crops! If it gets very rainy, or if it starts to frost, hold off on watering your garlic as it does not like being excessively wet. This can cause rot, and when the soil is very cold the garlic does not need additional watering. They love the cool temperatures and bright sunlight, and they will be sure to brighten up your pantry as long as you give them the love and care they need!

When the tops of your garlic plants begin to yellow, you can stop watering them. This means that it is the almost harvesting time! When the leaves get about one-third yellow, it's a good time to harvest the bulbs. Gently dig into the soil with your hands and pull out the root, careful not to snap the stem or tear the leaves as you do so. Never yank the garlic out by the stem as you would other root vegetables, for garlic is a bit more fragile than its brethren. Remove the garlic with the stem and leaves in-tact and you are good to go! Garlic does well in the curing process if it has its leaves and stems still attached, so it's a good idea to keep your garlic plant in one piece until you decide whether to dry or cure your crop.

If you do not prefer to use your garlic right off the bat, you can store your garlic. When you store it, it is best to cure, or dry, the crop first. Before taking this step, make sure to avoid washing your garlic with water as it is unnecessary and can cause your crops to rot. You can simply leave them as-is or brush them off with a dry cloth to remove excess dirt and debris.

When you cure your garlic, you will want to get all of the moisture out of the leaves, stem, and cloves. Allowing your garlic to properly dry will give it longer shelf life, and it will prevent damage, mold, and rot in the long-run. Hang the clover somewhere dark and dry in order to cure them well, and after two weeks or so the leaves will have completely dried. This will leave you with a delicious, ready-to-store, or eat product once you clip off the roots and the stem!

Leafy Greens

Spinach

Spinach was seemingly made for the container-gardening life, for it simply thrives in it. You can grow spinach in a shady corner, on your window sill, or just about anywhere with partial shade and moderate temperatures. Spinach is a staple in many healthy diets, and you can save heaps of money while reaping all of its nutritional benefits when you plant it yourself! It contains many powerful nutrients such as fiber and iron, and it tastes good to boot! This popular leafy green is delicious and can be eaten raw, like in salads and wraps, or boiled and served steaming-hot and mouthwatering!

Spinach is quite easy to grow in most sized containers, for its root system is shallow and hardy. Just keep in mind that the wider the container, the more room your spinach has to grow! Spinach is incredibly flexible and grows well in many soil types. It also does fairly well in different climates, but it prefers temperatures on the moderate-to-cool side of the spectrum. It does best in the very late winter or early spring once snow or frost begins to subside, and it can even do well inside the house most of the year as long as the house is kept nice and cool in the beginning.

Spinach is easy to harvest, as you just have to pluck or cut off leaves as you need them. Then, your spinach will continue to grow and flourish over time, and soon you will have a near-endless supply of the delicious leafy greens! You can choose a large variety of spinach, from the purple and green-leaved Japanese Spinach to the Giant Nobel, or even the Malabar. They all taste wonderful, and they are each unique and beautiful! You can't go wrong no matter which you choose!

Spinach loves the shade and it loves plenty of water! It goes well pretty much anywhere you choose to place it, and the mobility of a container makes it easy to adjust where it in for optimal growth! Many choose to keep these greens inside in a large pot, on the window sill in a small container, or outside among the shade of the trees. Wherever you choose to place your spinach plants, they will surely not let you down. Just make sure to keep them relatively cool so they give you the biggest and best leaves that they can, for if they get too warm they may begin to sprout and flower, which is not what you want from a leafy green plant that you'd like to eat.

To store your fresh spinach, keep it in an airtight plastic bag for a few days, but make sure to eat it soon or it may begin to wilt. Spinach generally does not last for more than a week, but as long as you like to eat spinach that won't be a problem at all!

Alternatively, you can dry your spinach leaves. This method will extend the shelf life exponentially, and you can grind the dried leaves into a nutritious powder that can be added to healthy smoothies, soups, stews, and savory biscuits!

Lettuce

The cool thing about lettuce is that there are so many varieties to choose from! It is also incredibly easy to grow in containers. From romaine to an iceberg, no lettuce will shy away from a cozy container home. In fact, some lettuce can even be grown in a small container of water in your very kitchen! This salad-loving leafy green is a must-have for those who love to add some lettuce leaves to their favorite sandwiches, salads, and burgers!

Lettuce thrives indoors and out due to its love of small, shady nooks and crannies. This leafy crop can grow just about anywhere with shade, and its shallow root system allows for any container size you have available to you. The bigger the container, however, the larger the head of lettuce!

The varieties of lettuce are nearly endless, and they come in beautiful colors from the classic green to the dark, maroon, and burgundy colors we know and love. There are also purples, reds, and more! Each type of lettuce has its own taste, texture, moisture content, and more, but anyone with a love for salads and greens will have a blast choosing the lettuce variety for their container garden.

The great thing about growing lettuce is that it doesn't really have to ripen, and it grows surprisingly fast! You can harvest leaves as you see fit, from smaller leaves to large, fully-matured heads of lettuce. They also love small spaces, and there are lighting preferences that can fit your home's environment as well. Most lettuce varieties like to chill out in the shade, but there are full-sun varieties as well. Whatever your preference, there is lettuce out there waiting for you!

Regardless of the variety of lettuce that you choose, these leafy greens are particularly hearty! They can withstand very cold temperatures up to warm temperatures, and they fit very well in the temperature ranges of spring and fall. However, you can grow them indoors during any season! As long as the temperatures in your home do not drop into freezing temperatures or soar to searing heights, as I'm sure they do not anyway, your lettuce will be right as rain! They can survive between the temperatures of around 45 degrees Fahrenheit to up to 85 degrees Fahrenheit! As long as you bring the lettuce inside or covered with a tarp during harsh frosts or particular hot spells, they will thrive with reckless abandon!

As for the watering of lettuce, you do not want to end up with soggy lettuce, so water lightly and frequently.

The best rule of thumb is to water your lettuce when you can feel the top inch or so of soil begin to get dry.

Kale

People normally either love kale or hate it, depending on their tastebuds. Kale tends to be a bit on the bitter side, but it is absolutely delicious when baked with a bit of sea salt and olive oil, and it is particularly good in salads. If you'd like to give this unique leafy green a try, it will definitely give you a healthy boost of vitamins and minerals, so they are a great green to cultivate.

Kale does very well in a pot or plastic container, and it is great for giving an added nutrient boost to your meals. These leafy greens grow large and bushy very quickly, and keeping a few of these plants around will fill your belly, and your nutrient quota, time and time again during continual harvest.

Kale enjoys a pot or container with a depth of about one foot, and they love well-drained but damp soil. This cousin of the cabbage comes in a very wide variety of colors and consistencies, and there is definitely a variety out there for you. There are vibrantly purple leaf and spear varieties, smooth, green plain-leaf kale, slightly ugly bumpy leaf kale, and more! Many of these types of kale are incredibly hearty and easy to grow.

Kale can be grown in much the same way as other leafy greens such as spinach and lettuce, and it loves water and cool oil. They do, however, enjoy sun more than their spinach cousins, so placing them in the partial sun is best. The sun will give them the spark of life they need, and the shade will allow for larger leaf growth. They need plenty of water to combat the heat, and with well-drained soil and partial shade that won't be hard to attain. They thrive in moist, cool environments, but they will do well indoors and out.

You can grow kale during a large fraction of the year, but they tend to be less productive in the heat of summer. For best results, when placed outside, fall and spring would be your best options.

When harvesting your kale, you can pick the leaves early or late, depending on your flavor and size preferences. Generally, smaller, younger leaves will give you a milder flavor with moist leaves, and larger, more mature leaves will give you a heartier, more flavorful result. Smaller leaves are often more tender as well, but you can gently massage larger leaves with your finger to soften them up. Adding a small amount of olive oil to your fingers will help even more when you massage the leaves, and removing hard stems and ribs will make the process even easier.

Larger leaves are generally more appealing for soups and salads, as they can be chopped or shredded for a nice, dense addition to dishes. Smaller leaves are often used for salads, wraps, and sandwiches.

To harvest, simply pinching or cutting the leaves off at the bottom will suffice. Make sure to leave enough of a stem for further growth, and you will be fine. Then, it is best to eat fresh kale within a day or two of picking, or you could dry it for longer storage. Kale baked in the oven with olive oil and sea salt makes for a lovely snack that will keep for a week or two as well. If you do store fresh kale, place it in a ziplock bag with a damp paper towel for the best results. Wait to wash any kale prior to serving it to prevent wilting.

Whether you bake, stew, or eat kale raw, this delightful leafy green will have a happy place in your container garden.

Pole Beans

Green Beans

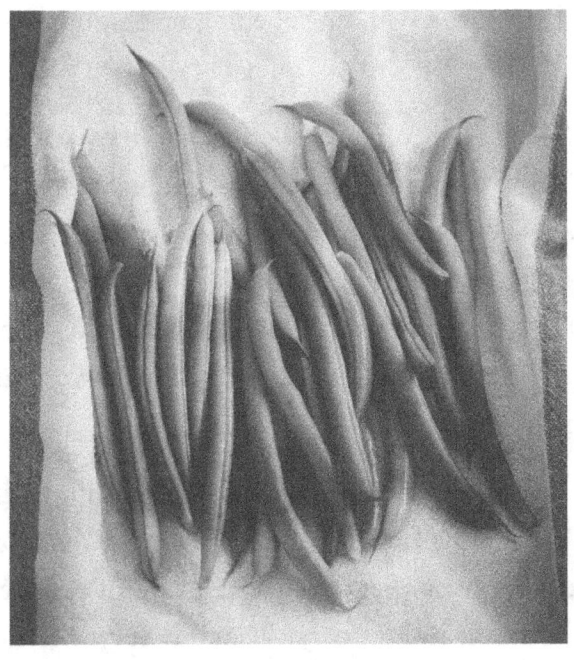

Pole beans, such as green beans, do very well in a container garden as long as they are supported by a sturdy wooden stake or a trellis. Aside from producing delicious, crisp beans for your favorite dishes, the green bean plant will create an aesthetically pleasing touch to your container garden. They crop lovely flowers and leaves, and they grow to an impressive size.

The best form of green bean to plant in a pot or other container is the bushy type of green bean. These need very little maintenance, and they thrive in this type of environment. There are also climbing beans, which are the ones that need a sturdy wooden stake in order to grow their vines without snapping or becoming entangled.

Green beans are very productive, and they will easily supply you with plentiful veggies to munch on and add to your salads and stews. They are very crisp and refreshing, and they are an incredibly easy plant to care for! They crop time and time again throughout the season, so you will have a very plentiful harvest full of green goodies!

Green beans have the advantage of versatility. They germinate and grow very quickly, and though you can quickly get overwhelmed by their rate of production, there is no need to worry! They do very well in the freezer, they are delicious when canned, and they are so delicious that you will eat them quickly with no problem! These beans are great for stockpiling during the year, and you will have plenty of veggies to last you through the chillier months of the year!

Green beans love the warmth and plentiful sunlight, and they can be easily grown in a container! The benefit of container-gardening with green beans is that they don't like to be transplanted, so you don't have to worry about moving these veggies from a pot to the ground because they don't prefer that method anyway! They enjoy a container depth of about one foot, and the bushy varieties may need a wider space to grow than the pole variety. Pole beans grow upward, so as long as you have a suitable pot depth and a tall stake or trellis, they will do just fine.

When you sow green bean seeds, they need to be watered, but if you water them too excessively, in the beginning, they can crack. If they crack, they may not be able to germinate properly, so make sure that your green beans have well-drained soil and plenty of sunlight. Adding mulch and compost helps the soil crop better-growing beans and less damaged roots.

Once the beans have sprouted, make sure they get plenty of water as they have shallow roots. Check the soil often and water it whenever the first inch or two of soil is dry. Green beans become plentiful quickly due to their amazing ability to self-pollinate. That means that they do not need the help of insects in order to crop crops! As long as your green beans have a sufficient amount of water and sunlight, they will bloom with reckless abandon all season long!

When watering your green beans, make sure to do so in the early morning. Many plants fare well when watered in the morning or evening, but green beans, in particular, prefer morning watering. This is because mold and unhealthy conditions can come about if the beans' soil is damp overnight.

Green beans are a wonderful, plentiful, and prosperous crop to grow in your budding container garden. They are perfect for beginners, and they can be perfect for you, too!

Herbs

All herbs do well in containers, but here are some of the most common household herbs that can be grown in containers inside and outside! We will be covering herbs with more depth in another chapter in this book, so this section will be brief, but it is important for me to showcase the wonderful option of planting herbs in your container garden in this chapter.

Basil

Basil is a delightful herb that goes very well in soups, stews, pizzas, sauces, and more! It pairs very well with tomatoes, which are another great container plant, and they are incredibly easy to grow and maintain! As an added bonus, basil makes a great companion plant for peppers and tomatoes, as it deters hornworms. Hornworms are a common tomato and pepper-eating pest, so basil can save your container garden! Basil loves sunlight, moderate temperatures, and well-drained soil.

Oregano

Oregano is another common household spice, and it is a staple in many homes. Oregano is great in just about anything, particularly sandwiches, pizzas, and soups! Oregano grows quite fast, so container gardening with oregano is the best way to control its rapid growth rate. Oregano basks in the sun and loves plenty of light, and it is very easy to take care of as long as they have sufficient light and occasional water. They don't need a lot of water, and they make great companion plants for other crops in your container garden, so you really can't go wrong with this lovely herb!

Sage

Not only is sage great in soups and when paired with meaty dishes, but when dried it can actually be burned for the purification of your home. Sage naturally purifies the air and has many antibacterial properties. Sage grows very well in containers indoors and out, and it is very hardy. Sage likes moderate temperatures and does not need much water. It is adapted to dryer areas, so occasional watering will suffice. If it starts to wilt a little bit, give it some water to make it perk back up! You generally only need to water sage when the soil begins to get particularly dry.

Parsley

Parsley is another household staple, and it is delicious with chicken, soups, and many pasta dishes! Parsley is wonderful to cook with fresh or dry, and you can't go wrong adding it to your garden. Parsley loves to be watered, and it thrives in well-drained, moist soil. It also likes to bask in the sun with minor to moderate shade.

Peppermint

The clean, fresh smell of peppermint reminds people of the holidays. It is lovely when brewed into teas, added to baked goods, and when hung up in your kitchen to dry! Peppermint permeates the air with a gently sweet smell, and it is a wonderful herb to have in the home and garden. Peppermint also acts as a natural repellent to many pests such as spiders! Peppermint does well in partial shade, and it likes being watered every other day in well-drained soil.

Rosemary

Rosemary is a kitchen's best friend, especially if you like to make baked and grilled chicken. Rosemary is very savory and adds a wonderful touch of flavor to any dish you pair it with! Rosemary does well in many environments, but it thrives in warmer, drier climates. The rosemary plant is considered an evergreen plant, so it is very hardy and lasts for a very long time indoors and out. Rosemary needs minimal water, as it does not like getting too wet, but keeping the soil relatively moist will give it the hydration it needs to survive.

Fruit

Berries

Many berries, such as blueberries, raspberries, and strawberries, do very well in a container garden! Even gooseberries make the cut! These delightful little fruits are useful in so many ways, from jams to jellies to pie fillings! They even make delicious garnishes on cakes, oatmeal, yogurt, and so many other types of dishes. What's better? They make beautiful additions to your container garden! With various, aesthetically pleasing flowers and colors, you really can't go wrong with a sweet berry plant in your garden.

An additional benefit to growing berries in your container garden is that pests are less likely to get to your fruit. This is especially prevalent in berries that you decide to grow indoors. Just keep in mind that nearly every berry variety enjoys ample sunlight. This is true for blueberries, raspberries, strawberries, and gooseberries.

When caring for your berries, it is important to water them often, as they have shallow roots. Water them whenever the top inch of their soil gets dry to ensure that they have ample hydration.

Cherries

Cherries are versatile and quite easy to care for in a container. You will have a plethora of cherries in no time as long as you care for your crops properly. The great thing about cherries is that they can grow from spring to autumn! They will give you all the fruit you need for spring tarts, summer pies, and autumn jellies!

Cherries come in two varieties, and those varieties include tart and sweet. Sweeter cherries enjoy lots of sunlight, and tart cherries prefer the shade. Both are delicious, and you cannot go wrong with either variety. Regardless of the type, however, make sure to give these shallow-rooted plants plenty of water to avoid wilting and decreased production. The best rule of thumb is to water them when the top inch of their soil gets dry.

Figs

Figs thrive in containers because their fruit grows much plumper when restricted by a container. Grown in the natural soil, the plant itself gets bigger, and the fruit does not have an environment in which it can grow to its fullest potential. By planting your figs in a container, they can grow much larger and become much sweeter than they would have ever had the chance to otherwise.

Additionally, figs love the sun! They love to bask in its light and warmth. If you give them a nice sunny spot in the house or an open and well-lit place outside, they will be quite pleased and crop great crops. It's a good idea to leave their container near a sunny wall or around warm rocks in full-sun so the heat will reflect onto the plants. They also enjoy being watered often, so make sure to water them at least twice a week for the best outcomes.

Figs do take a bit of patience, however, as they take about a year to fully crop. Planting these trees in the early fall will bring the best results, and you will have plump, juicy figs by the next summer! They grow their fruit in the spring, generally, and the fruit ripens to perfection by the end of summer. You can tell if a fig is ripe if you gently squeeze it and it is soft to the touch. If the skin splits a bit, that means they are fully ripe. The longer you let them ripen, the sweeter they will be. Good figs come to those who wait!

Plums

Plums are another great container-bound fruit, and they are absolutely juicy and delicious! The trick to growing plums is that they need a good drainage system for their roots. As long as your ads a bit of gravel or gritty material to the bottom of their container, and throughout the soil, they will do nicely. Water them when the top inch or two of soil is dry, and they will be content.

In Conclusion

Whether you choose beans, greens, berries, tomatoes, or any other crop on this list, you really can't go wrong with the delightful choices in this chapter! There is such a wide variety of plants that can be perfect for the unique container garden that you want to cultivate! Branching off from the choices here, even, are dozens of unique fruit and vegetable varieties that will leave you scrambling for more containers to fill. Take your pick and start growing all of the wonderful foods and spices that you desire!

CHAPTER 7: DIFFERENT VOLUME CONTAINERS

Though there is a nearly endless expanse of containers you can choose from for your garden, there are some parameters to keep in mind. Volume is the most important to consider depending on what you are planting. In this chapter, we will go over different plant types and the container sizes they generally need so you can choose the correctly-sized containers for your planned gardening space. We will take into account the general depth and volumes of containers dependent on plant and root types, as well as general sizes for plants that grow in various ways.

There is a bit of wiggle room with most plants, mind you, but this list will give you a good starting point for your gardening endeavors. You can, however, branch out and try new pots as you grow your garden and see what is right for you. Remember that the smaller the pot you have, the less the plant will grow, and the bigger the pot, the larger the plant will grow. This does not factor into the fruit size, however, so keep that in mind as well. For instance, figs enjoy a smaller space to grow in because their fruits grow larger that way. If they are in a larger space, their roots grow longer and the fruits are generally smaller. Every plant is unique, but as stated previously, this is a general list and can be modified as you go through the necessary trials and errors of gardening.

Shrubs and Trees

This category includes plants such as figs, which grow from a small tree, and plants that grow from a shrub, such as a blueberry bush. Generally, these plants enjoy a container volume of around **twenty to thirty gallons**.

Large or Climbing Fruits and Vegetables

Large fruits and veggies, such as tomatoes, bell peppers, chili peppers, and smaller berry bushes enjoy a container volume of approximately **ten gallons**. Pole beans, like green beans, enjoy these types of spaces as well.

Herbs and Greens

Many herbs, such as basil, sage, and parsley, enjoy a container volume of only **one or two gallons**. The same goes for leafy greens, such as kale and spinach, and lettuce varieties. The smallest containers that you have chosen for your container garden would be best suited for these leafy plants!

Grouped Fruits and Veggies

This category includes fruits and veggies that enjoy growing in a group, such as root vegetables, including radishes, beets, and onions, and small fruits like strawberries. With these plants, anything generally works. These plants can thrive in nearly **every size of the container**, just bear in mind that if it is very small, you will not get as much of a crop. The biggest factor to consider when planting these fruits and veggies is that simply need to make sure that you have the appropriate amount of space with which to space out your seeds. You also need something that is deep enough for the root growth of your plants, but fruits like strawberries have shallow roots, so it is not as much of an issue in that case.

In any case, depending on how well you can maintain your garden, or how much time you have, choosing a pot that is a bit larger is generally the best option. When in doubt, go a little bigger so you have some wiggle room for your plants. Plants can always live in a bigger pot, but if you go too small, they may not grow as well.

This guide gives a good, basic understanding of the ranges of container volume that are suitable for most plants, but it is always best to go with your cut and gauge the perfect size for your specific plants. Start with this guide and customize it to what fits your particular garden, and you will do wonderfully. Over the years, or even months, you will find what suits the health of your plants best.

Now that we have discussed volume, I will leave this chapter with a final note on container depth, which normally goes hand-in-hand with a container's volume. For your veggies, try to go with a container that has a depth of around eight to twelve inches regardless of the container's volume. This will allow your plant to grow tall and proud, while its roots happily thrive in the soil volume of your container. Herbs can live in a smaller depth, closer to six or eight inches, so keep that in mind as well.

I hope this chapter has given you a great overview and starting point for your container volume needs so you can cultivate a thriving and long-lasting container garden!

CHAPTER 8: GROWING AND HARVESTING VEGETABLE GARDEN & FRUITS CONTAINER

In this chapter, we will be going over some important factors of container gardening pertaining to the cultivation of your plants. This includes sowing, succession planting, harvesting, storing, and more! Later in this book, we will go into harvesting with more depth, but we will present a general overview in this chapter as well. The most important part of growing and harvesting your fruits and vegetables is the steps you take to prepare and maintain your garden. It is a delicate cycle that must be started with care and calculation. We will go over many of the steps that you will need to master in order to prepare and maintain your garden and your crops over time.

The unique aspects of container gardening lead it to require a bit more planning and preparation than simply planting your fruits and veggies in the ground. With container gardening, you have more control over the plant's specific environment, and you have to carefully choose its living space, soil, and more. With ground-gardening, the soil is already there for you to place your plants into unless you choose to add compost or other organic materials first. This is not the case with container gardening, but more on that later. Let's go over all of the steps that you need to follow in order to properly cultivate your perfect container garden.

Cultivating Your Container Garden

Preparing the Soil

Choosing and preparing the soil for your container garden is likely the most important step to cultivating your plants. As we've already discussed the selection of appropriately-volumed containers in the previous chapter, this is a section that is important to focus on. The plants that you add to your yard, ground-bound garden and more already have a stable soil foundation. The plants that you incorporate into your containers, however, do not have this luxury, and ground soil is not going to suit them in a contained environment. Because of this, you must select and prepare the best soil for their specific needs.

As natural soil is not geared toward your container-bound plants, you need to look for a better-suited solution. Most types of soil that you dig from the ground do not retain water as well, can crumble, and may contain unwanted pests. Many turn to commercial potting soils, which are a great option due to their specific manufacturing in favor of potted plants. These soils are packed with materials that will help aerate your soil, give it proper nutrients, and retain water for the roots of your plants. This is a very good option for nearly every plant that you store in a pot or other container since that is what it is made for. They normally have optimal nutrient and PH levels,

Alternatively, you can make your own potting soil right at home. If you like producing your own soil and do not want to rely on a commercial brand that you have no control over making, consider this option. It is important to ensure that the soil you make is lightweight enough for your containers, as you want to keep the plants healthy while keeping the ease of mobility for your containers. You also want to make sure that it will drain well. This is why commercial soils are normally easier to use, as getting the homemade mixture just right can be a bit tricky. However, given the right amount of dedication, you will do just fine if you would like to create potting soil on your own!

An important thing to keep in mind when preparing your own soil is its PH level. Most if not all potting soils should have a PH range between 5.5 and 7 unless you are growing a plant that prefers acidic soil. For the most part, this range will do just fine.

We will go over different ingredients for homemade soil in a moment, but here is a general overview of the soil-mixing process:

1. Place your ingredients together in a wheelbarrow or large container.
2. Mix the ingredients with your hands, if you have gloves on or a small shovel.
3. Add a bit of water to the mixture and stir it in.
4. Add the desired fertilizer and mix it in as well.
5. Add the soil to your containers and store the remainder of the soil in large Ziplock bags or in an unused, plastic trash can.

That's it! The best type of fertilizer to use in these mixtures, if you choose to do so, needs to contain vital plant nutrients such as potassium, nitrogen, limestone, calcium, and zinc. This will give your plants an extra punch of health that will spur their growth and crop better crops!

Now, let's get into the actual soil recipes so you can try out the mixing process above. I will go over three soil mixes here, each with their own benefits: Basic, Soil-based, and Bulb soil mixes. The basic soil mix is a well-rounded soil that is great for most plants. It has simple ingredients, including dirt from your own yard, that makes it easy to create and great for your gardening needs. You can add organic material to bulk it up if needed. The soil-based mix is best when you add fertilizer as an additive, and it is great for most plants as well. Bulb mix is necessary only for early forced bulbs, as it does not have enough nutritional content for most other plants.

Basic:

- 1 part sand
- 1 part ground-soil
- 1 part natural compost or peat moss

Soil-based:

- 1 part perlite or sand
- 1 part loam
- 1 part tree bark or peat moss

Bulb:

- 1 part of charcoal
- 2 parts shell, crushed

- 6 parts peat moss

Possible additions to any of the mixes mentioned include:

- Manure (this adds nutrients to the soil)
- Limestone chips (this helps reduce acidity and aids with the drainage of the soil)
- Sand (sand aids in the drainage of the soil)
- Perlite (this aerates the soil and improves its drainage abilities)
- Moss (moss is a great additive for retaining water)

With any of these soil mixtures, or with commercial potting soil, make sure to leave at least an inch of air above your soil in any container to allow for proper watering. If you fill your container too high with soil, it will cause the pot to overflow and wash out a lot of the soil. This can cause a big mess, not to mention erosion, poor water absorption, and more.

Once your plants die and it's time to change out the potting soil, if that occurs, it is not a good idea to reuse the old potting soil. Good reuse of this soil is to toss it into a compost pile, but in any case, used potting soil is normally devoid of any nutritional value it had at the start. This is because the plant that was in the soil likely soaked up all of the nutrients that it could while it was alive. If you must reuse potting soil, take out any roots, and mix it with either compost or new soil to bring back part of its nutritional value.

Fertilization

Fertilization is critical to the container garden cultivation process because plants that live in pots and containers retain fewer nutrients due to more frequent watering schedules. When you water your plant, nutrients drain out with the water, unlike ground-bound plants with ample soil that does not drain out nutrients. Therefore, you need to know how to properly fertilize your soil.

If you added fertilizer to your homemade or commercial soil when you first planted your crops, wait about three weeks before you begin the fertilization process. Additionally, the more frequently you water your plants, the sooner you will need to fertilize them. Generally, you need to add about a week's worth of fertilizer after two or three waterings to keep them up to par with nutrition. You can also fertilize once a week, depending on your plants. Keeping a gardening journal helps with this, as you can better gauge how well your plants do with a certain fertilization level over time.

With normal ground-based plants, you need to fertilize about once a month, but once or twice a week is needed for your container-bound plants. Generally, if you go by the one tablespoon per gallon monthly method, you will need to cut that in about one fourth for your weekly or twice-weekly fertilization.

If you don't like to schedule fertilization, or you do not prefer water-soluble fertilizer, you can add time-released fertilizer to your soil and mix it in, eliminating the need to schedule fertilization. With time-released fertilizer, it gets mixed right into the soil, and every time you water your plants, a sufficient amount of nutrients is released.

Whichever method you choose, it is always a good idea to keep your plants happy, healthy, and well-fed with the nutrients that they need.

Sowing/Planting

Whether you are sowing new seeds or planting saplings and young fruits and veggies, this is a very important step for container garden cultivation. You can buy plant-ready, premade plants that can be plopped right in a container without the need for sowing, or you can grow straight from the seeds. You can even propagate plants that you already have and plant them into a container to grow them from a parent plant. Whichever you choose, there are some tips that you will need going forward.

Here are a few great planting tips:

- Leave an inch or two between the soil level and the rim of the container to allow easy watering and unhindered growth for the plant.
- Beans, radishes, spinach, and kale are best grown from the seed rather than transplantation.
- Fertilizing the soil before sowing allows for faster germination and a kickstart to the growing process.
- If you are adding a new plant to your container, and not a seed, it is a good idea to loosen up the roots before placing the plant in the soil to promote root growth and branching.
- Thoroughly but carefully water the soil directly after adding your seeds or plants to settle them into their new home.
- Adding a bit of mulch will help keep the water in and prevent the plant from becoming unsettled or loose.

Succession Planting

Succession planting is a great way to boost the productivity of your container garden over time. When you use succession planting, you will eventually have a near-constant crop yield, whether it be herbs, fruits, veggies, or leafy greens. This form of planting involves an easy-to-follow system that allows you to use one container for multiple harvests.

This form of planting can help you reap the most benefits from changing seasons, weather fluctuations, and more. The process of succession planting basically involves incorporating two different types of plants into the same container. You choose one plant that has a certain seasonal harvesting time and maturation speed with another plant that has a near-opposite harvesting time and maturation speed. This allows for year-round harvesting from the same container at different times. For instance, you can plant a crop that is harvestable in the fall alongside one that is harvestable in the summer, so at the turn of the seasons, you have a crop waiting to be picked. On the other hand, you can have a plant that matures at a slow pace paired with one that rapidly matures so you can constantly harvest a crop while the other is coming to fruition. Root vegetables paired with pole beans and herbs do well with this method, such as carrots and basil or beets and green beans.

Another form of succession planting involves placing a very fast-maturing crop in a container and rapidly adding another plant as soon as that one matures. Basically, it is a quick replaceable method that allows you to always have a plan in motion.

To break it all down, here are three ways to look at succession planting:

1. Once frost season is over, plant a crop that matures well in warm seasons. As soon as its harvest is over, sow an autumn-loving plant that matures quickly.
2. At the beginning of spring, plant a crop that enjoys cool weather and matures quickly. Then, once you harvest this crop, plant a crop that enjoys warmer weather.
3. Plant a crop at the beginning of spring that prefers colder temperatures and matures quickly. Then, at the start of summer, plant a crop that prefers warmth. Lastly, in autumn, plant one last crop that enjoys cool weather.

These processes prove beneficial, but you have to stay on top of it. The timing of succession gardening is incredibly important. If you plant too early or too late, you won't get the proper maturity point at the time that you want. A good tip for succession gardening is to keep a well-marked calendar so you never miss the turn of a season. You can even color-code it for plant type!

Watering

Watering is by and for the most vital aspect of keeping your plants alive. This is particularly true in a container garden. Containers retain water less than the ground, so after the water has drained out of the pot and the roots suck up the hydration they need, it is not long before the plant needs more water. This is why it is critical to keep a detailed watering schedule for your plants.

Generally, plants need to be watered when the top inch or so of soil becomes dry. You can either go through all of your containers and feel the soil for yourself, or you can determine the watering needs for your plants and keep a detailed calendar so you know exactly when it is time to water the crops. Whichever works best for you, stick with it. There isn't really a wrong method here. You just have to make sure to keep up with watering your plants so they do not begin to wilt and die off.

When you schedule the watering of your plants, pay attention to the weather. If there is heavy rainfall, hold off on watering for a couple of days. If there is a particularly warm spell or a drought, you may want to water more frequently. Play it by ear and pay attention to the environment around you. Plants that are kept inside should have a fairly consistent schedule, but those plants that you keep outside need to have extra attention.

The best times to water your plants are the morning and evening, as the sun is not high during these times. In the middle of the day, or during any sunny parts of the day, the water in your container can be evaporated too quickly for your plants to benefit from the hydration. If you water during the early or later parts of the day, this is not a big problem. Make sure to water your plants until you start seeing a bit of water drain from the bottom, for this is a good indication that the entirety of the soil has been properly hydrated. Do not let the water spill over the top of the container, however. As long as you keep a good eye on the water and the soil as you hydrate your plants, you should be fine.

Harvesting

Once your crops have been cultivated and grown to perfection, there comes a time when you must harvest the fruits, or vegetables, of your labor! This is often the most exciting step to the gardening process, for you begin to see the benefits of your hard work. Harvesting times vary for each plant that you choose, and we will go over-harvesting in much more depth later on in this book, but let's go over some basics. As this is a very important and rewarding step in the gardening process, it deserves to be mentioned.

Harvesting for all intents and purposes occurs when necessary and when the plants are ready for your tastes. For instance, many plants can be harvested at different times, depending on the maturity levels that you prefer. A good example of this is the bell pepper. Bell peppers are able to be harvested as soon as they begin to fruit and turn plump and green. However, the longer they remain on the plant, the sweeter, and riper they become. They also get more colorful the longer they remain on the plant, with the exception of green bell peppers that are green at all stages. You can choose the maturity and sweetness levels of these crops as you see fit.

Another great example is spinach. When your spinach begins to grow, you can take the leaf off whenever they get large enough to eat. You can choose if you want small leaves, large leaves, or something in the middle. It is entirely up to you. That is the beauty of growing crops. You are in charge of the harvest, with respect to the seasons and maturation periods.

In any case, here are some great tips for harvesting in general. We will delve into the different plant types in the harvesting chapter of this book. For now, we'll divulge some useful advice for your harvesting seasons!

- Look at your seed packets and the tags that come with the plants that you purchase. This can give you a good indicator of general harvesting seasons and maturity levels for edible plants. It will give you a nice frame of reference for the amount of time you will have to wait before you can begin your harvest, and it will help you plan.
- Some plants crop what is called a continual harvest. These plants are great, for you can harvest them time and time again. For these plants, it is beneficial to harvest the crops faster to allow further crops to crop at a faster rate. Many plants, such as tomatoes, will continue to ripen

after you pick them, so if you time the harvests well, you can have quite the haul. Peppers, beans, and similar plants work the same way.

- There are certain crops, such as root vegetables, that do not get ripe. They are edible at any stage in their development, but it is up to you when you would like to harvest them. Generally, the longer you let them mature, the larger they will get. It is a matter of preference when you harvest these vegetables, as their taste sometimes changes with size. A great example of this is the carrot. There are baby carrots as well as fully grown carrots, and people prefer each for different reasons. You can get smaller carrots for salads and soups, or you can wait longer for a crunchy, full-grown root veggie.

Storing

Storing your fruits and veggies is the last step of a crop's life before you consume it. When storing, there are many options to choose from. Depending on the crop, some like to hang up and dry their veggies, such as garlic, chili peppers, and herbs; some like to store their crops in the refrigerator, such as lettuce, bell peppers, and berries; some like to put veggies in the cellar or in a bin of damp sand, such as with root veggies like beets and carrots; and some like to freeze their veggies, as with green beans and some peppers. Each storage option has its benefits and drawbacks, and many storage methods are crop-specific, but whichever you choose, storing your excess crop is a great idea if you do not plan to eat it for quite a while.

Another great option that many choose for veggies is canning. Green beans, beets, and more can enjoy years of shelf life in a can, and it is the preferred method of many gardeners that have a plentiful harvest. You can also sun-dry certain types of the crop for long shelf life, or you can store the crop right in your belly!

Regardless of your storage option, the best tip I can give to new gardeners is that when you harvest and begin to store your crop, *do not wash it off with water.* I repeat: Do not wash crop with water. You should always wash your crop with water right before you plant to eat or prepare it, but not anytime else. Water encourages mold growth and rot, and it does not bode well for stored fruits and veggies. If you must clean off some dirt, do so with a clean, dry rag. This will make it less messy to store your crop without letting in mold-inducing moisture.

CHAPTER 9: ACCESSORIES AND TOOLS

Container gardening is a delightful take on traditional gardening, and the great thing about it is that it's not rocket science! All you need are the right tools, information, and the right amount of dedication to kick container gardening out of the park! Read on for a comprehensive list and description of all the tools and accessories you will need in order to make the most of your container gardening experience!

The great thing about many of these tools is that you can improvise. You can also get very creative! For instance, instead of a dibber, which is a small device used for creating holes in the soil for seed planting, you can use your finger, a pencil, or any small, narrow stick. The same goes for containers and labeling methods, both of which have absolutely endless possibilities! Let's dive into this gardening toolbox to see what we can find that will help us take container gardening by storm!

Containers

Containers are the bread and butter of container gardening, as the name suggests. Your plants have to have a lovely place to call home, and containers are just that! The great thing about this tool is that the possibilities are endless! As long as the container is sturdy and has proper drainage potential, you can use just about anything! You can go with the traditional terra cotta pot, a big plastic tub, a DIY wooden gardening crate, and more! Some gardeners have gotten particularly creative and repurposed common household items, such as buckets, kitchen sinks, and even old boots! As simplistic or goofy as you want to get, there is always a container out there just for you!

When you choose your container, pick one that will go well with the space that you have and the general plant ideas that you have. Choose the plants that go well with the containers available to you, and plan out the layout of your container gardening space to get a good idea of your overall gardening goals.

Gardening Gloves

Gardening gloves are not necessary, but they definitely help! With gloves on, you get less dirt under your nails, have a softer surface with which to handle your plants, have protection against thorns, bugs, and dirt, and more! They also protect you from poison ivy, ants, and plants that you may be allergic to. Gloves also double as a great way to gently wipe dirt off of your veggies once you harvest them. This gardening staple is great to have in your toolbox, and you can go with a sturdier, rustic variety, or a nice, patterned pair of your choice! It's a good idea to have back-up pairs in case your gloves get very dirty, and having a few different varieties helps you tackle all of your gardening needs.

Garden Shears, Pruner, or Scissors

Garden shears, pruner, or scissors are great for clipping away vines that are getting too long, harvesting crops safely, and much more! They also help prune stems and branches, and they are great for any of your garden-trimming and harvesting needs! Make sure to keep your shears, scissors, or pruner sharp so they cut cleanly through your plant, and avoid dull blades for they could damage and bruise your precious plants. Rust-proof blades are also a plus. Pruners work very well for tomatoes, peppers, and more, and they will help keep your garden neat and your plants safe from damage and overgrowth!

Dibber or Small, Narrow Stick

Dibbers are small, narrow devices that are used to dig holes for the placement of seeds. They are quite useful for marking and digging places in the soil for perfect sowing, and they can be easily replaced by small sticks, pencils, or anything that is small and narrow enough to create a usable hole for your seeds or bulbs.

Mesh Sieve or Window Screen

Mesh sieves, or a window screen, are great for laying seeds, veggies, and roots out to dry. They are wonderful for washing off crop and seeds as well, for the water will easily drain through the small holes without any seeds or veggies falling through. You can place these sieves or screens on racks for better mobility and storage, and they are perfect for aerating your seeds and crop for optimal exposure to the air. They also conduct heat well, which is great for sun-drying.

Mason Jars, Paper Bags, and Ziplock Bags

When you have a prosperous container garden, you will likely have many crops that you need to store. That's where jars and bags come in! When you harvest your crops, you're going to need a place to put them! Mason jars work great for turnips, beets, green beans, and any veggie you'd like to pickle! Paper bags work well for storing garlic, and plastic bags are great for most veggies such as lettuce, beets, radishes, and more! Whatever you choose to use, you will definitely need these essential storage tools to keep your crops fresh and crisp!

String, Yarn, or Twine

String, yarn, and twine may not seem like gardening essentials, but they can help you in many ways once you begin container gardening. They can be used to tie and hang bundles of herbs or vegetables for drying, they can secure vines and stems to support stakes, and they can be used to hang your gardening tools! There are many possibilities, but string, yarn, and twine definitely have their place in your gardening toolbox!

Watering Can or Hose

Watering your container garden is essential, so you will definitely need tools that are up for the job! Watering cans come in a variety of shapes, colors, and sizes, and they are best for watering less hardy plants that need a gentle soak. Watering hoses are great for all-purpose watering, for they can have many differently pressured nozzles that can be utilized for your gardening needs. It's up to you which you choose for your watering needs, but generally, watering cans are more popular for smaller gardens and hoses are better for larger, more spaced out gardens.

Spade or Trowel

Spades and trowels are essential for transplanting your plants, digging holes for larger seeds and bulbs, leveling out soil, and more! The trowel and spade are both necessary for gardening, and they are very similar. The trowel is smaller than the spade, used for scooping and digging around smaller plants, and the larger spade is used for bigger containers and plants. Metal trowels and spades work much better than plastic ones, and they won't bend as easily.

Three-Pronged Fork, or Hand Cultivator

Hand cultivators, or three-pronged forks, are great for tilling the soil and gripping weeds. They also work as a tool for mixing fertilizer and compost into the soil. This is a great tool for container gardening, as it is much smaller than a rake or hoe, and it is easy to use! Metal hand cultivators or forks are best for all-purpose use, for they won't bend or break as easily.

Wooden Stakes or Trellises

For plants that need a bit more support, such as tomatoes, peppers, and pole beans, stakes and trellises are a must. Many plants with heavier fruit and long vines need to lean on these tools in order to stay healthy and prosperous! You can tie the plant stems to the wooden stakes, or allow vines to crawl up trellises, to keep your precious plants from bending and getting unruly. Plants that bend without support run the risk of damaging their stems and crushing leaves and crops. With a stake or trellis, this is not a problem!

Labeling Stakes, Paint, Markers, and/or Labeling Tape

When you have a garden full of various containers, it can get a bit hard to tell which plant is which. This can be easily solved with proper labeling, and it can be really fun to come up with creative solutions to this predicament. You can go with the traditional labeling stakes, complete with the names and possible pictures of the herb or veggie you're growing. You can also go with creative labeling tape for a removable method of marking. Or, you can tap into your crafty side and decorate your containers with paint and markers for a unique and beautiful design to tell the world just what you are growing! The sky is the limit, and you can use your imagination to make your container markers as beautiful or as simple as you like!

Kneeling Pad or Soft Towel

It's a good idea to have something soft to put under your knees when you are digging around in the dirt. This tool is not essential, but it certainly helps keep your knees clean and out of the rough dirt or gravel. It's easy to get tired out or scraped up when you are kneeling on the sidewalk, in the itchy grass, or in a big pile of dirt, so having something to keep your knees safe is a good idea. It will also double as something to sit on when you need to take a rest from gardening!

Tool Care Tips

Here are a few quick tips for caring for your tools so they will remain useful for years to come!

- Clean your metal tools often to keep them from getting worn out or dirty over time.
- Keep your metal tools nice and dry after cleaning them, and keep them out of the rain to prevent rust.
- Sharpen your scissors, shears, and/or pruner often to ensure that they do not get dull and damage your plants.

- Every month or so, it's a good idea to disinfect or sanitize your tools with rubbing alcohol or a bleach-water solution.
- Lubricate your shears, pruner, and scissors every once in a while to keep them running smoothly.
- Try to organize and store your tools in one space so you always know where everything is. This prevents them from getting lost or damaged. Great options are a small garden shed, peg-boards, shelves, a toolbox, or a series of hooks on the outside wall of the house.

CHAPTER 10: VEGETABLE & FRUIT GUIDE PER SEASON

The year is full of beautiful fruits, veggies, and more just waiting to be planted and harvested! When, however, can we see the results from all of our hard work? When can we plant our favorite fruits and veggies? These questions, and more, will be answered in this chapter. Here is a comprehensive list of the fruits, herbs, and veggies you can plant per season, as well as a list of the general harvesting seasons for each type of plant. The plants that are in bold can be planted year-round as long as there are not extreme temperatures such as negative temperatures or temperatures in the near-hundreds. They can also be harvested year-round, normally a month or two after planting, depending. I hope this list will help you determine what crops you would like to plant and when you can plant and harvest them.

Plant

Winter

- **Beets**
- **Bell peppers**
- **Kale**
- **Lettuce**
- **Onions**
- **Oregano**
- **Parsley**
- **Peppermint**
- **Radishes**
- **Rosemary**
- **Sage**
- **Spinach**

Spring

- **Beets**
- **Bell peppers**
- **Cherries**
- **Green beans**
- **Kale**
- **Lettuce**

- **Onions**
- **Oregano**
- **Parsley**
- **Peppermint**
- **Radishes**
- **Rosemary**
- **Sage**
- **Spinach**
- **Strawberries**

Summer

- **Basil**
- **Beets**
- **Bell peppers**
- **Cherries**
- **Chili peppers**
- **Figs**
- **Kale**
- **Garlic**
- **Green beans**
- **Lettuce**
- **Onions**
- **Oregano**
- **Parsley**

- **Peppermint**
- **Plums**
- **Radishes**
- **Rosemary**
- **Sage**
- **Spinach**
- **Tomatoes**
- **Most berries, including strawberries, raspberries, blackberries, gooseberries, and blueberries**

Fall

- **Beets**
- **Bell peppers**
- **Figs**
- **Garlic**
- **Ginger**
- **Green beans**
- **Kale**
- **Lettuce**
- **Onions**
- **Oregano**
- **Parsley**
- **Peppermint**

- **Radishes**
- **Rosemary**
- **Sage**
- **Spinach**

Harvest

Winter

- **Beets**
- **Bell peppers**
- **Kale**
- **Lettuce**
- **Onions**
- **Oregano**
- **Parsley**
- **Peppermint**
- **Radishes**
- **Rosemary**
- **Sage**
- **Spinach**

Spring

- **Beets**
- **Bell peppers**

- **Garlic**
- **Kale**
- **Lettuce**
- **Onions**
- **Oregano**
- **Parsley**
- **Peppermint**
- **Radishes**
- **Rosemary**
- **Sage**
- **Spinach**
- **Strawberries**

Summer

- **Basil**
- **Beets**
- **Bell peppers**
- **Blackberries**
- **Blueberries**
- **Cherries**
- **Chili peppers**
- **Figs**
- **Garlic**
- **Green beans**

- **Kale**
- **Lettuce**
- **Onions**
- **Oregano**
- **Parsley**
- **Peppermint**
- **Plums**
- **Radishes**
- **Raspberries**
- **Rosemary**
- **Sage**
- **Spinach**
- **Strawberries**
- **Tomatoes**

Fall

- **Basil**
- **Beets**
- **Bell peppers**
- **Chili peppers**
- **Garlic**
- **Ginger**
- **Green beans**
- **Kale**

- **Lettuce**
- **Onions**
- **Oregano**
- **Parsley**
- **Peppermint**
- **Radishes**
- **Raspberries**
- **Rosemary**
- **Sage**
- **Spinach**
- **Tomatoes**

CHAPTER 11: THE RIGHT POT FOR EVERY PLANT

Gardening is as much about planning ahead as it is maintaining it in the present. In order to get the best out of your gardening experience, plan out the spacing of your garden ahead of time, and plan the general size and material of the containers you'd like to disperse. This will make it easier to select the right seed or plant size so you can create the container garden of your dreams.

As a general rule, plants should be sized for their containers, and the containers should be sized based on the area at which you would like to grow them. By this, I mean if you have a larger area to grow your plants, you can have larger containers and thus a larger sized plant per container. If you have a smaller living space or yard, you can go with smaller pots that house smaller plants or herbs. It's all in the spacing and your plants of preference.

With that said, and with the chapter on pot volume in mind, let's go over some of the different types of pots that we may encounter when we plan out our garden. In general, any pot is good for your plants, as there is a large expanse of possibilities out there. Choosing the best pot for your plant is not a matter of if it will work, it's how. We will cover different materials that you generally see with gardening containers, and we will go over how to modify certain containers for things like drainage.

Once you have your pot size in mind, as aided by the container volume chapter, all you have to do is figure out what material, or aesthetic, you'd like to go with. Different materials have varying levels of price, durability, mobility, and more, so all of these factors must be considered before deciding on your garden's aesthetic. We will cover all of this going forward, so let's begin!

The Classic Clay Pot

Terracotta, or clay, seems to be one of the most popular pots on the market today. While they look nice and do the job well, it is important to note that clay pots break rather easily. They are not very durable when a plant grows very large, and they may break during heavy weather or animal involvement. If a clay pot falls over, it has a high probability of at least cracking. Additionally, clay pots are quite heavy, which makes it harder to move when full of soil and plant matter.

If you are sure that your plants are in a safe place without too much animal or weather interaction, they may be a good choice for your garden. This is especially true if you don't plan on moving your garden too much. Terracotta pots are also very inexpensive, so if budgeting is an issue, clay pots make a good choice for the wallet.

Another benefit to clay pots is their ability to retain heat. If you have plants that prefer lots of sunshine and warmth, these will make quite a suitable home. Take care, however, for in the warmer months of the year this can lead to more watering once the soil begins heating and evaporating water.

Metal Containers

Metal containers are quite versatile, as there are many types of metallic material that you can use to make a gardening pot or planter. The versatility of metal containers gives a gardener quite a plethora of options for their garden. There are lightweight metals, thicker, heavier, more durable metals, metals that rust and give a certain aesthetic to your garden, and so much more. It's a matter of shopping around and choosing the best type for your tastes and needs.

Bear in mind that many metal containers do not come with drainage holes, so you will need to take care of that yourself. In order to maintain the health of your plant and prevent root rot, drill a few holes at the bottom of any metal container you purchase if it does not already have them.

The types of metals used for containers are numerous, but the most common are copper, stainless steel, cast iron, aluminum, and iron. Steel and iron are the most likely in that list to rust over time with exposure to water, but if you like that look, it has its own place in a beautiful container garden. If you choose to paint your metal containers, it can reduce the risk of developing rust in the long run, so that is a great option as well.

If you go with a lightweight metal such as aluminum, take note that they have a tendency to dent easily. On the flip side, heavier metals like iron are much harder to move around, but they have heightened durability and rarely crack or dent. When you purchase a metal container, pick it up, and gauge your ability to move it to see if it is a good fit for your garden. All in all, metal containers are a great addition to a container garden, you just have to do a bit of research to see what kinds are the best fit for your style and personal gardening needs.

Fiberglass Containers

Fiberglass containers are very good at mimicking granite, stone, and ceramic pots while retaining durability. They are more lightweight than the aforementioned and mimicked materials, and they are quite weather-resistant. They do tend to have a thinner surface than other substances, however, and can crack if forcefully dropped. They make up for this by being weather-resistant and mobile, however, so they still make a great alternative to heavier materials. Aside from their durability, mobility, and lightweight material, they are not as popular as other lightweight materials due to their higher price point.

Fiberstone Containers

Fiberstone is a very unique and lightweight stone-substitute for a container. It is made by mixing fiberglass with limestone and a composite, and it looks just like stonework. The benefit of this type of container is that it looks just like a beautiful stone container while remaining light enough to move around with ease.

The walls of a fiberstone container are much thicker than that of fiberglass, which gives it an added layer of durability that is not found as often with a fiberglass container. They are also resistant to water, allowing ample moisture to get to your plants with no problem. They can be both indoor and outdoor containers, as they rarely crack under the pressure of weather or sunlight. These are among the best containers to use for your garden if you want something that will hold up over the years and is easy to move, but due to the quality and aesthetics of the material, it can be a pricy container to utilize.

Polystyrene Foam

Polystyrene foam containers are lightweight and mimic many other materials, such as stone, clay, porcelain, metal, and concrete. However, they can get pretty expensive, and they are not as durable as some of the other options on this list. They do a great job of providing a lighter alternative to heavier materials, but they miss the mark a bit due to their ability to chip over time. They are also a bit expensive.

Aside from the downfalls of polystyrene foam, these containers are great at insulating soil and roots, and they hold up against extreme temperatures. They are also very easy to move due to their light material, which lowers the risk of dropping and breaking them. If you have the room in your budget, these containers will serve you well. Just make sure they do not get dropped or knocked over, as their designs and decorative coatings can chip or dent easily.

Resin Containers

Resin is a substance that is made by pouring a polyethylene composite into a mold, which is then baked into the form of a container. These containers are quite versatile and can be made to look like a variety of materials. They can mimic concrete pots, stone, granite, and more. This gives them a chic and stony feel that is sought after by many contemporary gardeners.

The great thing about resin is that it is very hassle-free, with heightened durability that resists cracking and weathering. These pots are also very light, allowing them to be moved around quite easily without the fear of breaking them. They are absolutely great for someone who wants optimal durability with a very mobile pot due to its lightweight and strong material. They are also eco-friendly, as many resin containers are made from recycled goods.

Wooden Containers

Wooden containers, such as barrels, pallets, and crates, give your garden a lovely rustic charm. Wood is very affordable, and you can either build your own container or purchase a ready-made container for a reasonable price. These containers are popular for their looks and the natural aesthetic they give. They are also great for their drainage capabilities and will resist rot if you get wood that can resist the moisture, such as treated wood, cedar, locust, and redwood. Bear in mind that natural wood is much safer for the growth of edible plants, as treated wood often has chemical properties.

Wood is great for insulating your plants from the heat and cold, and it will last many years before having to be replaced. They also have natural cracks and slats that allow for ample water drainage, which makes them great for plants that are susceptible to root rot. If you are going for a woodsy charm in your garden, these containers will make a great addition to your home. They can be painted in a variety of beautiful colors and patterns, so you can get whatever look you like!

Fabric Containers

Fabric containers are a wonderful alternative to the more mainstream gardening containers on the market today, and they are easy on the wallet. These containers are among the most lightweight of gardening containers, and they aerate the soil and roots very well. These containers often come with handles, but with or without these additions, they are incredibly easy to carry and move from place to place. This is great for plants that need to frequently be moved in an out of the sun, and they are wonderful for when you'd like to do a bit of garden reorganization!

The greatest, arguably, the benefit to fabric containers is how well they support the roots of your plants. They prevent a condition called root circling, and they allow for easy transplanting as the roots to not go through the fabric. This container facilitates a complex branching network of roots in your plant, preventing them from tangling and circling around. This makes it hard to remove a plant from a container, and thankfully, fabric containers give optimal mobility and transplantability to your plants.

You can grow anything from trees to small plants in a fabric container, and they are well-ventilated and temperature regulated due to the nature of the fabric. They come in many sizes and colors, so it is easy to find one that will suit your needs.

Ceramic Containers

Ceramic containers come in a variety of shapes, colors, patterns, and sizes which gives them a very aesthetically pleasing potential. They are quite beautiful, but that beauty comes with a price in the container gardening realm. Ceramic containers are very hard to move around due to their heavyweight, and worse yet, they break very easily. This wouldn't be as much of a problem if they weren't expensive, as made apparent by their artistic designs, but this does pose a dilemma. You are essentially sacrificing durability for beauty. Ceramic containers crack very easily under the pressure of weight, temperature changes, and impact. They crack very commonly in the winter if left outside.

If you choose ceramic pots for the beauty they will bring to your garden, and you have the budget to do so, then, by all means, you can go with this form of container. Just bear in mind that if you want durability, mobility, and a budget-friendly method of plant containment, this is probably not the best fit for your garden.

I will say that ceramic containers hold moisture well, as they are less porous than other container types, such as clay. Therefore, they can benefit plants that need more hydration than others. That, paired with their beautiful decorative capabilities, makes them valued as gardening containers if you have the budget for them.

Concrete Containers

Concrete is one of the heaviest materials used for container gardening, but it is also quite durable. If you do not plan on moving your plants often, this may be a good idea. However, due to their weight, if you have plans to rearrange your garden at any time, it can be very difficult to move your concrete-bound plants.

Concrete is waterproof and resistant to weather, and it breaks rarely. It is also quite affordable, but you won't really be able to move it once you pick a spot for it, so plan ahead. If you want something that does not hurt the budget, insulates your plants, and won't topple over during a storm, this may be the pot for you.

Hypertufa Containers

Hypertufa is a great choice if you like concrete but do not like its immovability. Hypertufa is much lighter than concrete, but it retains a lot of the durability and the look of the heavier material. As an added plus, it is frost-proof. Hypertufa is created from a mixture of Portland cement, perlite, and peat moss. It is not very expensive, as it can be made right from home, so it could be a great choice for those who like to dabble in DIY projects.

Fiber-lined Containers

Fiber-lined containers are normally metal or wire-framed containers that are lined with a fibrous material that is either made from coconuts or synthetic materials. These are popular for hanging plants such as ivy and flowers, but it has been seen with container gardening edible plants as well. Common examples of this container type are railing planters, hanging baskets, and porch planters. There are many other examples as well, but these are the most common.

Fiber-lined containers are wonderful for a variety of reasons. Hanging planters allow for your plants to remain safe from ground-dwelling pests, and it removes the fear of flooding or pot-tipping. Fiber-lined containers also have amazing drain ability, which is wonderful for preventing root rot. You will need to water plants in these containers often, however, as they dry out much quicker than other container types. A good way to combat this is to put plastic lining, or even plastic wrap, between the soil and fibrous material. Just make sure to poke holes in the plastic for drainage.

These planters are not very expensive, and they have a variety of uses for any garden. They are also considerably lightweight and mobile, so you can change up your garden design any time that you need to. They look very natural and blend in with most yards, which is very nice for those who want a subtle but pleasing look to their garden.

Plastic Containers

Plastic containers are among the most popular and least expensive of all container types, and they are highly recommended for any gardening need you may have. They come in any color you can think of, and some actually mimic more expensive container varieties. They are very durable and rarely crack under the pressure of temperature and the weather, and they tend to be one of the most lightweight materials you can use to contain your plants.

Plastic containers are highly recommended if you want something that looks very nice in the garden while not hurting your budget. They come in many sizes, fitting any plant you choose to incorporate into your garden.

The only downside to plastic containers is that they tend to fade in color over time, but this can be easily fixed with a fresh coat of paint. They hold moisture in very well, and for the most part, they come with drainage holes in the bottom. If you have a plastic container without drainage holes, all you have to do is cut or drill holes in the bottom and it will be fine. Drilling or cutting holes in plastic is much easier than doing so with a material that will crack easily, such as ceramic or terracotta. This gives you the power to utilize the plastic to whatever drainage needs you may have.

If plastic containers fall from a considerable height, or too much force is placed upon them, they may crack, but they are a lot more resilient than materials like clay, glass, and porcelain. It would take nearly twice the force, if not more, to crack plastic than it would crack the more fragile materials I've mentioned. All in all, plastic is a well-rounded, beneficial material with which to contain your plants.

Miscellaneous and Unique Containers

If you want to go outside the realm of normal gardening, this section is for you. I'm looking at you, the kitchen sink. Unique containers that are repurposed for the use of gardening can be some of the most fun containers to use for your garden. This can be anything from a big pair of old boots to a kitchen sink, as mentioned, to something as bizarre as an old bathtub or wheelbarrow. They can be as expensive or inexpensive as you need, as you can recycle old items or pick something up from an antique store.

No matter what container type you choose, there is something for everyone! Try one or try them all, it is completely up to you. You can have one wooden container and a dozen clay pots, a fabric container, and a kitchen sink, or a plethora of plastic. Whatever works best for you will be what is best for your garden! Experiment, get creative, and have the best time designing the container garden of your dreams!

Parameters to Consider

Drainage

Drainage is very important for any container that you choose to garden with. Whether it is a natural pot or a strange, repurposed item, you need to make sure it has drain ability. Your plants have to be able to use up the water they need and expel the water that they don't in order to prevent root rot.

This is as simple as checking the bottom of your container for drainage holes before using it, and safely adding holes to the bottom if it does not have any already. Most commercial garden pots and containers have pre-drilled holes, but if you are using unconventional means of plant containment, you'll need to add them yourself. The exception to this is if you use something such as a colander, sink, bathtub, or other items that have some form of a hole in the bottom already.

Another great step to take would be to add a few rocks to the bottom of your container before adding the soil in for a boost to your container's drainage abilities. Just make sure the rocks don't deter the water's ability to drain through the appropriate drainage holes.

Durability

Regardless of the material you choose to go with, you need to make sure it will be durable enough to withstand plant growth, weather, and a variety of other factors.

Weight and Mobility

One of the greatest advantages of a container garden is its ability to be modified, moved around, and flexible. You want the containers that you use to reflect that. It is much easier to rearrange your container garden if you choose containers made from lightweight, but durable, materials. This ensures that your plants are happy in their homes while having the ability to be moved as needed.

CHAPTER 12:
SELECTING SEEDS

Selecting the seeds for your garden can be a very exciting experience when you start your journey into container gardening. However, it can also be quite daunting! Never fear, however, because in this chapter I will help break the process down to make it easier for you. We will go over making a seed-buying plan, choosing the right variety of seeds, go over a list of possible places to purchase your seeds, and discuss the storage of your seeds for the next year. Without further ado, let's get started!

Create a Plan

Before you purchase and select your seeds, make a rough diagram of your container garden and create dots in all of your containers to see how many seeds you need for each, and what type. This helps create a visual that will allow you to purchase exactly how many seeds you need and which kind. It helps you avoid overspending or underspending on your seeds, and you end up with the perfect amount for each crop.

For instance, if you would like to plant lettuce, kale, and green beans, you could plan it out accordingly. Let's say you want one container for lettuce, one for kale, and two for green beans. Generally, lettuce containers contain six seeds, evenly spaced out into two columns. Kale, on the other hand, needs only one seed in its container to sprout a crop, and green beans require around eight to nine seeds spaced evenly in columns throughout the container. Keeping this in mind, you can draw out a diagram with one lettuce container holding six seeds, one kale container holding one seed, and two containers of green beans holding roughly eight seeds each. When you take a quick glance at the diagram, you simply have to count the dots to see how much you need to purchase for a specific growing season. In this case, the total would come out to around twenty-three seeds total.

Creating a great visual, and a plan is a wonderful first step in the seed selection process. It will give you a bearing on how many, and of what type, of seeds that you will need to purchase. Granted, my example is on a smaller scale for simplicity, and purchasing a simple handful of seeds per crop is not likely for avid growers, but it gives a good starting point to look at.

Choosing the Right Seeds

Seeds are very easy to find, and they are available to purchase at many retailers, nurseries, home improvement stores, and more. However, how do we know what differentiates good seeds from the bad? Most of the time, you can find relatively inexpensive packs of seeds at the store in little packets, or if you want to go with bulk seeds, it can be a bit pricier upfront, but cheaper in the long run. Whichever size you choose is up to you, but either way, you need to find quality seeds that fit your budget and your gardening needs! Generally, buying seeds from any of these places will give you great crops, and it is mostly a matter of budget and specific plant varieties that will steer the path of your decision. You can also take into consideration whether the seeds are from organic plants, GMO or non-GMO sources, and more.

Here is a list of some places you can find seeds for your garden:

- Retail Stores, Home Improvement Stores, and General Stores
- Nurseries
- Seed Swaps
- Online Retailers

Now that you know where you could potentially look for your seeds, let's dive into what could be on the labels of these seeds so you know that you are buying the ones that are right for your health and garden. Generally, seeds are labeled one of three ways: GMO, hybrid, or open-pollinated. We will discuss each of these so you know what you are getting into when you peruse the packaging on your seed options. We will also toss around other terms you may find in your seed-searching journeys, such as organic and heirloom.

Before we delve into the three seed types, let's go over the words I mentioned just now. The terms heirloom and organic will likely show up on many seed labels, depending on their type. Any seed that has the word heirloom associated with it simply means that the seeds come from a long line of other plants. A generation, so to speak, or many consecutive generations. Heirloom seeds are seeds that have been passed down from one crop of plants to the next, grown carefully for the preservation of its beneficial qualities. An heirloom seed is generally a good-quality seed, as the gardeners have preserved the best parts of its past generations.

The term organic on a seed label means that the seeds were harvested from the organic crop. This is a positive term, for organic plants are strictly regulated to avoid

GMOs, harmful chemicals, and a number of other malicious cultivation means. If you see a label on a seed packet that says conventional, that means that it is not an organic variety of seed. Now that we've discussed the term organic, let's dive into its opposite, GMO.

GMO is something that I would strongly advise against. GMO seeds pertain to plants that are genetically modified, and they are not natural. GMO seeds, and subsequently plants, hold less nutritional value than organic or naturally-grown varieties, so they will not give you the best results nutritionally or, arguably, taste-wise. GMO plants are entirely manmade, scientifically altered, and not created the way the earth originally intended. GMO plants can have genes spliced from fish, bacteria, and other foreign organisms. Many argue that GMO plants were created to give added benefits to consumers, such as natural pesticides and resistances, but they generally do not fit the bill of health. Once more, I would strongly advise against this type of seed, regardless of the price point. Thankfully, GMO seeds are not as common in most container-friendly plants, so it will not be difficult to find non-GMO seed varieties at your store of choice.

Hybrid seeds are also manmade, at times, but in a much less harmful way than GMO seeds. They are wildly different, in fact. Hybrid seeds can be created by man or nature, and are simply a cross between two different species of similar plants. For instance, a hybrid seed could come from the cross-pollination of two different tomato plants, thus creating a new form of tomato brought about by the pairing. This pollination can be human-caused or nature-caused, but the results remain similar. When it comes to the labeling of a seed packet, generally hybrid means that the seed was created by human means and deliberate cross-pollination. The difference between hybrids and GMOs is that hybrid plants are created from natural cross-pollination and not genetic splicing, and the hybrid is always the result of two different plants. No foreign genes are introduced, as seen with GMOs, such as frog genes and other unexplainable additives. Human cross-pollination is normally not harmful to plants and mimics the work of many insects, such as bees. Most humans take a soft brush and move pollen from one plant onto another, facilitating natural processes that create the seeds you will be purchasing.

Last but not least are open-pollinated seeds. These seeds are created in a very natural setting, normally without the participation of human hands. Open-pollinated seeds are created by insects, weather, or birds that spread pollen throughout the land and create seeds in the aftermath. These seeds are generally more expensive, as they are not mass-produced or influenced by humans. They are randomly and wildly created by nature, which is very exciting! Open-pollinated seeds create many heirloom varieties, due to the close quarters of similar plants that crop the next generation of offspring. Hybrids can also be created naturally this way, as a bee can buzz along and pollinate a pumpkin with a neighboring zucchini plant and create a spray of newly-created seeds and crops! The rarity and value of the plants created to lead to individual pricings and overall plant values, but these seeds are a wonderful and completely natural option for those who want to let mother nature do the work.

Storing Your Seeds

If you store your extra seeds correctly and plan to plant the same crops the next year or two, you can save a heap of money in the years to come. Seed storing is not difficult at all, and you can even harvest seeds from your mature crops to save even more money! To store your seeds, all you really have to do is put them in an airtight container, such as a mason jar with a lid, and store them in a dark, and dry, environment. You can keep them in the pantry for future use, in a cabinet, in your closet, or anywhere that is dark! Some people even store their seeds in the refrigerator, as it is a dark and well-preserved space. Wherever you choose to store your seeds is a matter of personal preference. Just remember to always keep them dry to prevent accidental sprouting!

CHAPTER 13: PROTECTING YOUR PLANTS

Once you have the container garden of your dreams set up and ready to grow, it is natural to worry about natural roadblocks that may get in your, and your plants', way of thriving. This is a common fear, but there are many ways to combat it! Protecting your plants is very important, and in this chapter, we will go over some of the most common gardening threats and how to solve each one. Read on to get a wealth of informational armor to defend your plants against any obstacle or critter that can come about!

Weeds

One of the great things about container gardens is that plants housed in containers rarely get excessive weeds. However, weeds have the potential to pose a threat if not monitored, like tree nuts, dandelion seeds, and more could drift or fall into your pots depending on the placement of your containers. Weeding is not hard to do for container-bound plants, though, as weeds are normally minimal and take only a brief moment to tug them out of the container.

To prevent weeds, you can situate your containers under the shade but not directly under trees to prevent acorns and such from falling into them. You can also bring your plants inside for a period of time during autumn, as this is a common time of year for acorns and other tree nuts to fall down.

Weather

Frost

The best way to keep your plants safe from frost is to cover them with a frost-protecting blanket, insulated plastic season extenders, or a large garbage bag. All of these options work, and it is a matter of what is easiest for you to master and afford. For frost-protecting blankets, you simply wrap it around the plant and container, or cover it in some cases, and tie the bottom to keep it from lifting off in the wind. With insulated plastic season extenders, they act like a form of mini, temporary greenhouse. Most fill with a bit of water and warm your plants, but the instructions vary. Check the packaging of your season extender for the best instructions. Garbage bags are likely the cheapest and easiest to utilize, for you just take an everyday plastic garbage bag and drape it over the entirety of your plant. Then, you weight the bottoms of the bag down with rocks or similarly heavy items. Each of these options will work well to keep frost away from your precious plants.

Drought

When it comes to drought, the best offense is a good defense. Prevent the over-drying of your plants' soil by adding mulch to the top of the soil. This helps your plant retain water and adds a layer of protection against the sun's heat. Another great way to combat drought is to water your plants more often during hot spells of weather. This will ensure that they have optimal amounts of water, especially if you water them in the early morning or late evening when the sun is not beaming down.

If you would like to add an extra helping of protection to your plants, there are commercial water storing crystals that retain water during drought and prevent over-watering by absorbing excess water. It's the best of both worlds, and it could save you a lot of headaches in the long run if you don't mind the extra expense.

Heavy Rain, Wind, and/or Thunderstorms

The best way to protect your plants during damaging and thunderous storms is to cover them with a larger container, overturned, and bring them under an awning or structure for added protection. This prevents the containers from tipping over, the leaves from being damaged, and the soil from washing out. Make sure to add something heavy, like a rock or brick, on top of the overturned container to hold it in place, and your containers will be safe and sound. Just remember to remove the weights and overturned containers after the storm so your plants can get much-needed sunlight.

Animals

It's natural for animals to get a bit curious when new crops start to grow. It can be a bit of a headache, though, when your newly-grown head of lettuce gets chewed up by a furry friend. There are many ways to combat this problem, however, so never fear! Your plants can survive the ravenous fuzzy animals if you put some of these protective measures into place:

1. Plant herbs, such as sage, lavender, rosemary, oregano, and more to naturally and humanely deter animals such as deer from your garden.

They do not like these smells, and it will mask the smell of your larger crops. Most herbs will do.

2. Set up a fence. Fences, whether small or large, keep out small and large animals from your container gardening area. It can be anything from a small wire fence to a large, wooden enclosure, but generally, a height of at least three feet is needed to keep out larger animals. Check often for holes and cracks in the fence, however, for it may need mending over time. Additionally, you will need to make sure your fence is planted firmly in the dirt at least once inch deep to keep out burrowing rodents such as moles.

3. Another solution is to surround your plants, especially climbing ones like tomatoes and peppers, in chicken wire. This adds a great layer of protection around them while giving them room to grow. This is particularly useful against squirrels and birds.

4. You can also use urine to pour around the perimeter of your garden, but this is normally a last resort. You can purchase predator, normally wolf, urine online, or at some gardening stores. This gives off a smell that scares off deer and

small animals when they fear that a predator is around.
5. Get a cat. Cats are natural predators to many small rodents, and they can deter these animals simply by being present near the plants.

General Tiny Insects and Pests

Aphids, among other tiny pests, are all too common to the gardening community. They eat away at your leaves, veggies, and more, and they can ruin the hard work that you've spent so much time putting into your garden. Never fear, however! There are plenty of ways to deter tiny pests, and they are not difficult to master.

1. Introduce predatory insects. These insects will not munch away at your hard work, but they *will* munch away at the insects that do. Such beneficial insects include ladybugs, wasps, lacewings, and more. Many of these bugs will naturally occur where the food source is, so if you have a pest problem, they will follow soon. However, you don't want to wait around while the pests eat away at your crops, do you? No. That's why you can attract beneficial critters by planting butterfly bushes and other plants that

they prefer. You can also buy ladybugs in certain gardening stores.

2. Cover your plants. Covering your plants with a lightweight, floating row cover can prevent bugs from getting to your crops. These act much like a mosquito net, and they are made with a spun fabric that is made specifically for this purpose. Simply place it over your plants and secure it, taking it off when the pollination season occurs.

3. Plant companion plants. By planting varieties of flowers and herbs near your container plants, you can deter harmful bugs and make it harder for them to find and eat your plants. Dill is a great example of this, as is lavender, peppermint, and more.

4. Deter slugs with sweet gum tree balls. These keep slugs away from your crops while not directly harming the critters, so it is a nice and humane way to keep the slimy fellas out of your crops.

5. I saved the best for last since it is likely the most important tip on this list. Do not reuse soil year after year. When you do this, any bugs that may be hiding in the soil, or their eggs, can get reintroduced to your crops over and over again. It is

always best to start fresh and eliminate this potential gardening hazard. Additionally, clean out your containers thoroughly between every planting change.

Hornworm Infestations

Hornworms are a particular concern for those who are growing what we call fruit vegetables, such as tomatoes, sweet bell peppers, and chili peppers. I am giving these bugs their own section of this chapter due to how commonly they plague many gardeners. They often lay their eggs in the soil nearby, and the larvae feed on the fruit of your plants. They can go unnoticed at first due to their small size and green coloring, but once they start chowing down on your precious tomato plants they begin to grow to astonishing sizes.

When this happens, it's not hard to spot these vermin among the stems and fruits of your plants. They can eat very quickly through your vegetables once they get to a medium-to-large size, and they can decimate your crop if you do not handle the issue early-on. Thankfully, I will give you some great tips on how to both avoid and irradicate this hornworm issue in a way that is humane and will not cause harm to your plants or the hornworms!

Handpicking

Handpicking hornworms from your plants may seem tedious, but it is the easiest and most humane way to rid the garden of these pests. Hornworms are harmless to humans, and though their spiny rear ends may look threatening, they pose no such threat to us. When you see one of these green worms, simply pluck it off with glove-covered hands to safely remove them from your plants. Then, you can gently place them in the grass or on a plant a safe distance from your garden.

It can take a while to find and pluck away all of these worms, but it will be the best way to keep the plants and the insects safe. The worms will scurry off, and your vegetables will be pest-free. Just make sure to come back every day or so to ensure that the hornworm population in your garden has not become a problem once more. As long as you are in the garden often, as you likely will be while tending to your plants, it won't be difficult to pluck off a worm or two while pruning, harvesting, and watering your plants.

Planting Basil

Another great and humane way to keep hornworms out of your garden is to plant basil alongside the vegetables. This is a preventative measure, as you should plant the basil at the same time as the tomatoes, for the scent of the herb will mask the smell of the tomatoes and drive away hornworms during their mating and nesting season. As an additional bonus, you get some wonderful, fragrant fresh basil to harvest right along with your tomato plants. They will both grow just in time to make some homemade tomato basil soup! It's a win-win situation.

If a few hornworms brave their way through the basil, you can still pluck the stray worms off your plants and send them packing!

Introducing Ladybugs

Last but not least, ladybugs are natural predators for hornworms. This may seem a bit odd, as hornworms can grow much larger than a ladybug, but it's true! Ladybugs feed on the eggs and larvae of hornworms, thus preventing larger hornworms from returning or growing in your garden. This method may seem less humane than the others, but it is part of the natural circle of life. Ladybugs naturally eat the larvae and eggs of many other insects, and you can introduce these lovely bugs into your garden for a hornworm-free experience.

CHAPTER 14:
HOW TO HARVEST

Harvesting is one of the loveliest aspects of gardening, and that is because you finally get to reap what you have sown! Each type of plant that we have discussed throughout this book generally needs to be harvested in a different way. We will go over all of our plant types in this chapter and discuss the best ways to harvest each one!

'Fruit' Vegetables

'Fruit' vegetables, such as tomatoes, bell peppers, and chili peppers, are quite easy to harvest. Once they have ripened, they normally showcase vibrant red, yellow, and/or green colors. Tomatoes, for instance, normally turn a nice, bright shade of red. This, or slightly before this, a showcase of color is when it is best to harvest them.

Tomatoes, and many other vegetables, continue to ripen after being harvested, so if you choose to harvest your tomatoes while they are still a bit yellow or green, rest assured that they will ripen overtime on their own. It is actually good to do this, depending on your preferences, as it encourages faster growth for future harvests.

Bell peppers are generally the same, but you can harvest them at any time once they begin to mature. Usually, the longer they remain on the plant to mature, the sweeter they will be. Therefore, it is up to your discretion and personal tastes when to harvest them.

With any of these marvelous veggies, you can harvest them easily. All you have to do is pluck them off their plants and carefully place them in your basket, bag, or whatever receptacle you are placing them into. If they are particularly tough to take off the plant, you can always use a pair of sharp scissors or a knife to cut them off safely.

Pole Beans

Pole beans, such as green beans, need to be harvested when they are around five to seven inches in length, or when they just the right level of thickness. You can normally tell when a green bean is thick enough to harvest, but it is important to note that when the beans inside begin to swell, they are slightly past their harvesting maturity. A good middle ground is the best way to go with these beans. Not too thick, as the beans will swell, but not too frail either.

Harvesting these beans once they reach maturity is a fairly simple task. All you have to do is tug them lightly to get them off their plant or pinch the area where the bean pod meats the plant. After that, you are good to go!

Root Vegetables

For most root vegetables, such as beets and radishes, harvesting is as easy as tugging the roots up out of the ground at the base of their leaves. If you are concerned about the greens being damaged or tearing from the root, simply dig around the base of the root and move the dirt around to loosen it up. Then, carefully tug out the root and you have your crops!

With most root vegetables, the time at which you harvest them is completely up to you! As soon as the roots begin to grow and mature, you can harvest them at any time. Generally, a moderate to medium size is best, as roots that get too large can begin to lose their taste. The best way to tell if a root vegetable is ready to harvest is when the root begins to crown over the top of the soil. This is generally the best time to harvest, but again, it is up to your discretion.

The best time to harvest your roots is in the morning. This allows you to get the vegetables out of the ground before the sun begins to beat down on you, and the drier soil is normally easier to work with. The dry soil loosens up a bit faster than moistened soil, and it does not clump up as much. This allows you to get your veggies out of the ground without too much of a mess or hassle. The sun also causes the leaves to wilt a bit when it is high in the sky, making them more frail and prone to damage during harvest.

Leafy Greens

For leafy greens like spinach, kale, and lettuce, harvesting is quite simple! Due to the fact that you are going to be eating the leaves of these plants, harvesting is entirely up to you! As soon as you see the leaves growing, you can start harvesting. It's all a matter of how big you'd like your leaves to be.

When you harvest your greens, it is best to go from the perimeter inward. This allows you to get the most mature greens first, from the outer areas of the plant, so the smaller, innermost leaves can continue to grow and crop. Simply pluck or cut the leaves at their base, and you are good to go!

If you would like a larger harvest, you can cut all the leaves down to the base, and you will have all the greens that you need. As long as you leave enough of the plant to see about an inch above the container of growth, it will continue to grow and crop after the harvest. After using this method, it will take a week or two before you can harvest the greens again.

Herbs

Herbs are much like leafy greens in that you are generally eating or using the leaves and stems. Generally, you want to harvest these by cutting the stems with a sharp knife. The best way to cut these plants is to leave about three or four inches from the base so the plant can continue to grow after harvest. Simply trim away the pieces that you will be using or storing, then let the rest of the plant continue to grow. Additionally, with more leafy herbs like basil, you can simply pinch off the leaves you would like to harvest and leave the rest of the stem and plant to continue producing more leaves.

You will know when it is time to harvest when the leaves become larger and more mature. The stems will have also grown long enough to leave about three inches from the base after harvest. If the plant begins to bud or flower, simply cut off the tips with the flowers to encourage further herb growth. The plant will continue producing long after you snip the stem, so you will have a continual supply of your favorite herbs over time.

Berries

Berries are among the easiest crops to harvest, for you simply have to pluck the ripe fruit from their plants! It is quite easy to tell when to harvest these plants, for you will notice the fruit gaining color and plumpness right before it is the optimal time to harvest them. You will want to make sure that the berry is completely uniform in color before you harvest it to ensure ripeness. For example, a strawberry should be uniformly red, and a blueberry should be uniformly blueish-purple.

With strawberries, you will want to keep the stem attached, so plucking them while pinching or snipping the stem is best. Smaller berries, such as raspberries and blueberries, fall easily off the plant into your hand. These do not require the stem to be attached, so pluck away with reckless abandon! Just make sure not to damage or crush the berries in the process. The easier these berries are to take off the plant, the riper they generally are.

The exceptions to the uniformly-colored berry rule are gooseberries and blackberries. To prevent your blackberries from being sour, it is best to not pick them when they are glossy and black. This coloration may seem appealing, but the berries become much sweeter when they begin to dull in color. On the flip side, gooseberries are optimally harvested just prior to their most ripened state. Gooseberries should be picked when they still appear slightly green, though some tend to wait until they get a bit pink.

Fruit

Fruit, such as figs and plums, that live in our container gardens are generally most mature when they are soft to the touch. This ensures that they are nice and juicy, and they will likely be much sweeter than the tougher, sour flavor they would have if they were not fully ripe. For plums, in particular, the darkened color of their fruit is another great indicator of harvest.

When you harvest these delectable fruits, take care not to bruise them. Particularly for figs, if you handle them too roughly, their skin may split and the fruit can bruise. Cutting the fruit from the stem with sharp scissors is the best route, as it does not require as much tugging as the hand-picking method. This method also allows the fruit to go a bit longer without spoiling as well, as fruit spoil at a slower pace when they have their stems attached.

With plums, in particular, another harvesting method is to gently grasp the fruit and twist it off of its stem. This requires minimal handling of the fruit before it is harvested, and it does not cause as much tugging or bruising.

A final and important note to fruit harvesting as it applies to figs is to always wear gloves. This is particularly true if you have a latex allergy, as fig stems and leaves secrete a milky-white liquid that contains fig latex. This liquid can cause itching and irritation to the skin of those with a latex allergy. When in doubt, wear gloves.

Drying out Your Herbs and Small Vegetables

Drying out your herbs and small vegetables after harvest is a great way to preserve your crops. For herbs, all you have to do is tie the bases of the stems together with some twine, sewing thread, or a small string. Then, hang them up to dry! The same goes for chili peppers and similar crops. When the vegetables, or the leaves for herbs, start to get dry and potentially crumbly, the drying process is complete!

For garlic and other root veggies, it is best to gently brush off any dirt, then trim the roots at the bottom of the bulb. After this step, tie the stems together and hang the garlic bulbs up to dry.

CHAPTER 15: MAINTAINING YOUR VEGETABLE GARDEN YEAR AFTER YEAR

Now that we have learned to grow, cultivate, sow, water, harvest, protect, and store our plants, we are near the end of our container gardening journey! However, before I leave you with our last chapters of knowledge, I'd like to impart some important maintenance tips for your garden so you can continue to thrive and grow year after year! In this chapter, we will go over some general maintenance tips that will help your garden thrive for years to come, and it will impart you with the knowledge that you can carry with you to every season of your gardening journey!

Mulch is a Wonderful Thing

While your plants are still growing and producing throughout the change of the seasons, mulching your soil is a great idea. It allows your soil to retain moisture, stay insulated, and protect itself against weeds. It also adds to the overall nutritional quality of your soil. Adding one and a half to two inches of mulch to your containers every year after you plant allows your garden to have a great foundation to grow from in the year to come. You will start off every year on the right foot if you add mulch to your itinerary.

Remove Dead Plants and Debris

Removing dead plants when they are finished producing, and removing random debris throughout the year, will keep your garden clean and manageable throughout the year and into the next year. It gives you more ease as you transition from season to season, and it allows your gardening experience to be much more clean and orderly. Do the same with weeds and random tree nuts to prevent unwanted growth in your plants' containers.

Additionally, while your plants are still growing, it is a good idea to trim off the dead plants and flowers to allow the optimal amounts of growth throughout the year. This is a process called deadheading, and it is critical to promoting the overall growth of your plants and garden as a whole. It also makes your garden much prettier to look at, which is always a plus!

This is all incredibly important to your garden's life for many reasons, but a little-known reason is that it helps prevent pests! The more dead matter and debris that litters your containers, the more inviting hiding spaces crop up for pests. Many insects are drawn to dead matter, as insects are natural scavengers, so clean away this possibility by removing dead matter from your garden. It also leaves the pests with nowhere to hide, so locating vermin gets much easier for you in the long run.

Check Up on Your Plants Often

Throughout the year, it is always best to check up on your plants. This allows you to regularly look for pests, diseases, and more that can carry into the next year if left unchecked. It is also important to check up on your plants to prevent serious damage from an otherwise unseen issue.

Keep a mark on your calendar or watering schedule every week so you remember to check your plants regularly for issues. If you do this, it will gradually become a habit that you can use in the following years of your gardening journey. This will benefit your garden as a whole over time. Additionally, it is a good idea to treat your plants for issues as soon as they crop up to avoid further issues down the road. If you find an issue, once it is resolved to try to put preventative measures in place to keep it from happening the next year. For instance, if you have a particularly bad hornworm problem in your tomato population, consider planting basil alongside it the next year to deter them.

Utilize Crop Rotation

Crop rotation allows your soil to remain healthy year after year if you choose to reuse and create your own potting soil. It allows nutrients to be replenished with intermittent plants like legumes and clover, and it will help you have an added boost for the next seasons to come. It is an incredibly important step to take if you plan to reuse pots and/or soil, so planning it out and utilizing it every year can give you a great head start for the years to come.

The reason that crop rotation is so important is that when you plant the same plant in one spot time and time again, it can leech the nutrients from the soil and encourage pests the recognize where their favorite vegetables are. Throw the pests off the trail and boost your nutritional values at the same time by rotating crops every other season or year.

Clean and Maintain Your Tools and Containers Every Year

Keeping your tools and containers clean after every season eliminates the threat of pests and diseases from being passed on to your garden in the next year. If you do this, it also makes your tools and containers easier to use. Dirt is a given in any gardening situation, but if you let it continually build up and cake onto your tools year after year, it can become a hindrance.

The best thing to do is to clean your tools once or twice a month, disinfecting them of diseases and debris on a regular basis. Then, whenever you change out a plant in a container or discard the soil, thoroughly clean the container and check for bugs, then disinfect it. After you disinfect it, rinse it off completely and allow it to air-dry before using it again.

Utilizing these tasks often prevents the spread of diseases and pests, and it will save you a lot of headaches over time. Make it second nature to routinely clean your equipment, and it will soon come with ease!

Read Over Your Gardening Journal and Learn From it

Reading over your detailed gardening logs from the previous year greatly prepares you for the next year to come. You will gain insight into the tips that you have discovered during the year, and you will learn from past mistakes. You can build upon this knowledge and grow from it year after year, and you can continue to keep a detailed log in the years to come.

Pruning is Critical

If you plan to keep a certain crop going through the turn of the year, and if you have dormant plants that you wish to come back the next year, it is important to prune them back to foster growth. Pruning your plants and cutting the branches or stems back allows for healthy growth once the new season begins. If you do this, it will allow larger and more prosperous plants to grow back, and you will have greater overall gains in the new year.

Another benefit of pruning is that it keeps your garden manageable over the years. If you allow your garden to get overgrown, it becomes increasingly difficult to manage and keep healthy month after month. Save yourself a lot of headaches and maintain your garden as you go to prevent more work in the future.

End the Year with a Nutrition Boost

Once all of your harvesting for the year is done, and after all of your plants have died off or been removed, it is prime time to prepare for the year to come. When your containers are properly prepared with soil, after you have cleaned them out, cover the soil in compost and mulch to allow it to steep in nutrition until it is time to plant once more. This will give your soil a large boost that will give you a head start once the sowing season begins once more.

CHAPTER 16: PLANT AROMATIC HERBS FOR YOUR KITCHEN

One of the best types of container gardening for someone who loves to cook and spend time in the kitchen is herb gardening. When you keep an aromatic herb garden in your kitchen, it gives your entire home a wonderful, inviting, and earthy smell. It also gives you easy access to herbs that you can pluck straight from your windowsill to use in your daily life. What can be more lovely than that?

Let's go over the ins and outs of planting aromatic herbs for your kitchen, then we will dive into some herbs that are specifically wonderful to keep around in a kitchen environment. Herbs are incredibly rewarding as a plant that you grow in your home, and you will soon see why with the lovely aromas they respond with after the minimal but loving care that you give them.

Start with Plants, Not Seeds

For the most successful indoor herb garden, you will want to purchase your herbs when that is already in plant-form. This makes it easier to get a quick yield of herbs, and it makes it easier to maintain, grow, and harvest them over time. Cultivating herbs from seeds in an indoor environment can be pretty tricky, so in order to make the most of your aromatic herb-gardening experience, plants are normally best.

There is a large number of plants that thrive in an indoor environment, so the transition from store to kitchen will not be too rough on these hardy plants. You just need a spark of passion for these plants, and a lot of care, and they will thrive from under your fingertips in no time! With your established plants in hand, you will be months ahead of seed-starting outdoor gardeners, and you will have delightful herbs for your kitchen in a manageable amount of time.

Pick the Right Containers

We know all about the importance of choosing the correct containers for your plants' thanks to the previous chapters, but it is uniquely important for your indoor herb garden. Not only do you want the right container sizes for your herbs, but you also need to make sure that the containers fit the style of your home while also supporting the amount of space that you have.

Generally, most herbs require a container with at least six inches of depth to promote healthy growth. Just make sure that it has sufficient drainage for watering, and the rest is mainly up to you. Map out the layout of your kitchen and select containers that fit the area and aesthetic needs of your environment. When in doubt, and if space allows, always aim a bit larger than the plant's minimal needs so they have room to grow and develop. This will ensure the greatest outcomes for your plants, and the greatest gains for you.

Group the Herbs in Your Kitchen By Their Needs

When growing aromatic herbs in your garden, it is best to group them together based on their needs. Then, give them designated spaces in which to grow side-by-side, giving a fragrant and beautiful aesthetic to your home. For instance, group sun-loving herbs together on the windowsill. Place shade-loving herbs in the corner of the counter or in another shady, designated space. House your partial-sun herbs on the counter near the window but against the wall of the counter for a nice, sleek look. Give each group of herbs their designated home, and you will all be happy as can be!

Growing Herbs in Your Kitchen Allows You to Harvest as Needed

The best part of growing herbs in your own kitchen is the ease at which you can pluck off a few leaves and toss them into your meals. When you have your own aromatic herb garden, you can have ready-to-use herbs at your fingertips at a moment's notice. Simply pluck off some leaves or snip some stems, rinse them in water, and you are good to go! It doesn't get much better than that, now does it? Simply wait until your herbs begin to grow their leaves and have established stems, then you can harvest as needed. Leave a couple of inches of the stem in-tact to promote further growth, but aside from that, you can harvest as much as you need!

Hang Herbs in Your Kitchen to Dry Before Storing

By hanging your harvested herbs in the kitchen before you begin to store them for future use, you add an extra boost of fragrance to your kitchen by allowing easy access to the herbs for cooking and other uses! Simply tie the stems together with a small string and hang over the window sill, on a nail in the wall, or in another open and dry place of the kitchen. This will allow them to dry perfectly and give you the best outcome for your culinary herbs!

The Best Herbs for Your Kitchen Containers

Now, let's get to the best part of this chapter: The herbs! Here, I will list the best aromatic herbs that are well-suited for a container-bound environment in the kitchen. There are many other useful herbs for the kitchen as well, but they do not do as well in an indoor environment, so for the purposes of this chapter, we will focus on herbs that grow well indoors. Without further ado, let's meet the herbs!

Basil

Basil is a wonderful and versatile herb to grow in your kitchen's garden, as it can be used in many dishes! Basil pairs wonderfully in many tomato dishes, and it also tastes wonderful in pasta and soups. Basil can be harvested by plucking off leaves and either drying them for seasoning or used fresh in dishes for a more poignant taste. There are many varieties of basil to choose from, which adds to its versatility as well. This herb has the classic basil taste, but also comes in spicy varieties and citrusy ones!

Bay

Bay leaves are often used in soups as a burst of flavor, but they have various uses in other dishes as well. These leaves grow a bit slowly, but they pick up as they become bushy and long. It may be a good idea to purchase an already established plant to give you a nice head start for your kitchen. Simply pull off leaves as needed and add them to your favorite dishes for a wonderful dash of flavor!

Chives

Chives give you a nice oniony flavor without the onions, and they taste great in soups, potatoes, and many meat dishes. They generally prefer a place on a sunny windowsill, and they can be harvested by cutting the leaves down to the base of the soil with a small segment left for regrowth.

Dill

Dill is one herb that simply thrives in an indoor environment. It has a distinct and delicious aroma that smells much like a pickle, but regardless of its aroma, it grows at a rapid pace indoors and supplies its grower with the best leaves for use in dishes. Dill tastes lovely on sandwiches and in many soups, and it has a taste that anyone can recognize!

Oregano

Oregano is a classic herb that gives off a nice flavor and smell. It is a common spice for sandwiches, soups, and just about anything you can think of. Its leaves grow quickly and need to be harvested frequently for new growth to be encouraged. Simply pluck the leaves off and add them to almost anything for a whirlwind of amazing flavor!

Parsley

Parsley is a favorite in the herb-growing world for pairing quite well with pasta when fresh, and quite well with just about anything else when dried. It has a mild flavor that goes well with many dishes, so it is a staple in many kitchens. The best part is that it loves being grown indoors. It has a strong flavor and aroma that permeate the air with aromatic glory, and it is quite easy to harvest. Simply cut the leaves from the outer perimeter of the plant to encourage new growth and get your flavor kick for the day. Parsley lasts for many months, so you will have a delicious and aromatic plant for a long time if you choose parsley!

Peppermint

Peppermint is one of the most aromatic and lovely herbs on this list for a number of reasons. For one, it smells wonderful and clean, and it livens up a room with its calming smell. Secondly, peppermint tastes amazing in many baked dishes, in tea, and as a flavoring. Thirdly, did you know that peppermint wards off bugs like spiders? That is a top-notch reason to keep it in a kitchen, in my opinion! Keep peppermint in its own space, in partial sun, for the best results, for it grows quite rapidly and can overshadow some of your other plants if left unchecked.

Sage

Sage pairs very well with meaty dishes and soups, and it grows to about one foot in height. Simply harvest this herb by pinching or cutting off the leaves, then add it to your favorite dishes for a burst of flavor. Additionally, you can harvest from the stem up for the best luck with hanging and drying the herb. Sage is beneficial for use in the home as a cleansing element. When dried and hung in the home, the scent of sage is said to cleanse the air of the home and remove many ailments and negative air pollutants.

CHAPTER 17: PROBLEM SOLVING AND FAQS

No matter how much you love gardening, or how much you know, there are some common questions that are sure to come up at some point in your container gardening journey. I am here to shed some light on some of your puzzling questions, and I hope that this chapter will make it a bit easier to get over your gardening obstacles! Read on to find some answers to the most common container gardening questions.

What *Is* Container Gardening?

This is, believe it or not, a very common question for gardeners. Never fear, however, for the answer is quite simple! Container gardening is for all intents and purposes the gardening of plants that are housed in containers! These containers can be pots, buckets, barrels, or even kitchen sinks! The possibilities are endless, but one thing remains the same: The plants live in a container!

Can I Use Any Container for my Garden?

Yes and no. You can be as creative as you like with the containers in your garden, and there are nearly endless possibilities, but there are a few factors to keep in mind when selecting the perfect pot or bucket. First, you need to make sure the container is sturdy enough to withstand the weather, weight, and moisture of your plants. You also need to make sure the container is durable enough to not be permeated by the roots of your plants.

Next, make sure that the container has proper drainage capabilities to prevent flooding and root rot for your vegetables, herbs, greens, and more. This part is fairly easy to fix, as you only need to drill a few holes in the bottom of your container to make it drainable. However, certain materials such as porcelain and glass break easily and aren't as durable as other options. These may not be good for draining the moisture in the soil. There are exceptions to everything, however, so trial and error is always your best bet! If you find something that looks particularly aesthetically pleasing but is not drainable, you can always nest drainable containers inside your container of choice to retain the look but maintain the health of your plant.

If I Don't Like My Container After a While, Can I Move my Plant to a New Container?

Transplanting any plant is generally frowned upon unless it is necessary. Moving a plant from one container to another causes unnecessary stress to your plant, and it can reduce the productivity and health of your plant to the point where transplanting isn't really worth it. A great alternative for this is to place your plant, in its container, inside an even bigger, more aesthetically pleasing container. This gives you the results you want without harming your plant.

Another option is to decorate your container! A fresh coat of paint does wonders for the look of your container of choice, and it can give you something new to look at! Make sure to choose a weather-resistant, waterproof paint so your new decoration does not fade or get damaged over time.

Is PH Level Important in a Container Garden?

Yes! Plants all need a proper PH balance, but thankfully, many commercial potting soils are specifically manufactured to be a sufficient PH level for many plants. Most plants like a PH range of about 6.2 to 6.8 and many commercial potting soils are in this range. Check the packaging to make sure, and research the PH requirements for the plants you are intending to grow for the best results.

Can I use Dirt from my Yard in my Container Garden?

The dirt from your yard, depending on where you live, is generally not recommended for container gardening. Naturally occurring soil in your yard is not sufficient for the drainage needs of your plants, and it may clump and flood more frequently than commercially-made potting soils. It is normally best to go with a commercial soil made specifically for pots and containers to ensure that your plants are given the nutrients and drainage capabilities that they need. You can also mix in organic compost for an added boost of nutrients and water retention!

Can I Water my Plants on the Same Schedule?

It depends on the plants that you are growing, but generally, each type of plant has a different level of water that is needed in order to survive. It is a common rule of thumb that container-bound plants need more frequent watering than the plants in your yard for the simple fact that pots drain out excess water, while the ground retains and disperses water more naturally than a closed-in pot. If your pot does not drain, it can cause root rot, so frequent, light watering is usually best. Research the watering needs of each plant you pick for your garden and write out a watering schedule for the best results and minimal confusion.

Should I Line my Containers with Rocks or Other Materials?

Yes! Lining the bottom of your containers allows for optimal draining and the least amount of root rot. Materials such as foam or packing peanuts are normally best for container gardening for lightweight padding that allows for easier movement of your containers. Rocks were well also, but they are much heavier and will make mobility a bit more challenging for your plants.

For shallow-rooted plants, fill your containers about halfway with your rocks or foam, and fill about an inch or two from the bottom for longer-rooted plants for the best results. Padding your containers with these materials allows for better root stability and easier drain ability, so it is always a good idea to go this route for the overall health of your plants.

Can I Have an Inside Container Garden?

Absolutely! Container gardening can be personalized to your needs, and some, like those who live in apartments, need a way to grow quality crop in the comfort of their homes. Thankfully, there are many plant varieties that work for indoor living. Generally, plants that like shade or partial shade are best for indoor gardening, as there is less access to light inside many homes. However, if you have a particularly sunny home with lots of windows, full-sun plants may be viable as well!

Generally, the best plants for indoor container gardening include:

- Herbs, such as sage, rosemary, parsley, basil, and mint

- Chili peppers, such as jalapenos
- Greens, such as spinach and kale
- Root vegetables such as radishes, garlic, and green onions
- Tomatoes
- Ginger root

What are Some Common Container Gardening Mistakes?

Mistakes are a given with any gardening experience, and practice definitely makes perfect. Here are some common container gardening mistakes that need to be avoided to make your garden prosper to the best of its ability:

- Insufficient sunlight
- Not enough water
- Too much water
- Improper drainage
- Transplanting
- Using soil from your yard rather than potting soil
- Not researching your plant before choosing it for your garden

CONCLUSION

Thank you from the bottom of my heart for reading *Book Title*. A lot of heart, soul, and information was put into this book, and I certainly hope that you gained a bushel of helpful information for your container gardening journey! I sincerely believe that you can conquer your container garden with the guidance of this book and that you can grow the most prosperous garden you can hope to achieve as long as you put in as much dedication and heart as I strived to incorporate into this book.

In this book, we discuss the many wondrous aspects of a container gardening endeavor, and we traversed the dangerous waters of pest control, frost prevention, seed selection, and much more throughout these chapters. We also reviewed some helpful tips and tricks for the gardening world, as well as guides for seasonal planting, choosing the perfect crops for you, maintaining your wonderful container garden through the years, planning out your perfect gardening space, and so much more.

I have provided these tools for you in the hopes that you will create a healthy and bountiful life for yourself and your family, and the information therein was specifically picked in order to help anyone with a green thumb find joy in the wonderful world of container gardening. I developed this content with the intent to expand the reaches of gardening to anyone who wants to create their own little garden, regardless of the space they live in. Anyone can container garden if they want to, and that's the beauty of it! Whether you live in a small apartment or a spacious mansion, everyone can benefit from a container garden!

I hope you can take this information with you and thrive with it, creating the container garden of your dreams. Take the next step in your plant-rich journey and cultivate a bountiful garden of your own! I hope that you will share this book with your friends and family so they can gain a wonderful tool for sustainable living in any space!

I would like to leave you with a final, hopeful note. If you enjoyed this book and gained helpful insight from its contents, please leave a kind and honest review on Amazon so I can reflect upon the constructive criticism or inspired testimonials from my readers. I greatly appreciate it, and it helps me develop greater content for the future! Thank you again for choosing my book out of the plethora of gardening books on the market today, and I sincerely hope it serves you well. I wish you all the best in your container gardening endeavors! Happy planting!

www.ingramcontent.com/pod-product-compliance
Lightning Source LLC
Chambersburg PA
CBHW071826080526
44589CB00012B/933